Elizabeth Taylor

TRIBUTE TO A LEGEND

BOZE HADLEIGH

GUILFORD, CONNECTICUT

For Ronnie

An imprint of Globe Pequot

Distributed by NATIONAL BOOK NETWORK

Copyright © 2017 by Boze Hadleigh

British Library Cataloguing in Publication Information available

Library of Congress Cataloging-in-Publication Data available

ISBN 978-1-4930-3105-4 (hardcover)
ISBN 978-1-4930-3106-1 (e-book)

∞™ The paper used in this publication meets the minimum requirements of American National Standard for Information Sciences—Permanence of Paper for Printed Library Materials, ANSI/NISO Z39.48-1992.

Printed in the United States of America

CONTENTS

PROD. 1315
ELISABETH
TAYLOR
#11 SCHOOL
DOG CART
BARN
BROWN HOM

"One of my most favorite fragrances is [Elizabeth Taylor's] Violet Eyes. Now you can also buy violet contact lenses!"   —Charo, Spanish comedian-singer-guitarist

"The word 'spectacular' has the same root as spectator.
It means to look. Elizabeth Taylor was typically a spectacle to behold.
Or else she was making a spectacle of herself."
—British actress Stephanie Beacham

"Her life became a continuing soap opera, but because it was real and so full of glamour, wealth, and romance, not to mention controversy, it was more interesting than any TV soap opera."   —publicist Dale Olson

"Fifty percent of all box-office income in 1966–67 was made from movies starring one or other or both Elizabeth Taylor and Richard Burton."   —film distributor Harry Walders

"She was in the news constantly during her two marriages to Richard Burton. But she was hardly unpublicized before him. Or after him. Elizabeth attracted publicity like a magnet."   —Jane Fonda

"At least one of her marriages was publicity-oriented—to politico John Warner. She later said it had been a mistake . . . they differed so much. For all her ultra-feminine display, Elizabeth Taylor was very strong. Regardless, Warner banned any reference to the Equal Rights Amendment during his campaign, of which his wife was the centerpiece."
—journalist Shana Alexander

"A woman like you could probably help get me elected senator."
—John Warner's pre-ET proposal to Barbara Walters, which she declined

"The Taylor-Warner relationship could be interpreted as pro-celebrity from both sides. He won his race with her help. And she, middle-aged and no longer a Hollywood lead, went east for a new spotlight and a temporary career as Mrs. Politician . . . and got fat in the process. Then she divorced, lost the fat, regained her looks, and started over again. People were agog." —*Entertainment Tonight* writer Wayne Warga

"So the irony is that Senator John Warner, thanks to a pro-gay, somewhat pro-feminist celebrity, is in office for thirty years and gets to vote against gay rights and women's rights. That is extremely ironic."
—*Who's Afraid of Virginia Woolf?* playwright Edward Albee

"Liz Taylor is the most publicized movie star of them all. Marilyn would compete for the title, except she didn't live long enough. The other contender is Garbo, but she avoided publicity and retired early, even though unwanted publicity continued to pursue her."
—film historian Douglas Whitney

"Her timing was very lucky indeed. Had she been born ten years earlier, or even six like Marilyn Monroe, the Fisher-Reynolds scandal would have stopped Taylor's career cold. Contrariwise, had Monroe been born six or ten years later and lived, she could have transitioned to a dramatic actress less dependent on her sex appeal."
—Creative Artists Agency (CAA) agent Rick Marroquin

"In the 1950s and into the '60s Marilyn Monroe and Elizabeth Taylor were roundly criticized by the media and 'morality' groups. In different ways, for different reasons. Marilyn for being too sexy and turning the male public on too much. Liz for being too sexual and aggressive in turning specific men on too much, taking them away from their wives and kids. You can see in retrospect that Marilyn did nothing wrong. She was blameless. Liz Taylor did bust up some famous households."
 —Susan Strasberg, actress and daughter of Marilyn Monroe's acting coach, Lee Strasberg

"She was one of the great beauties of history, and played some of the great beauties of history. She was criticized for both . . . I don't think if Elizabeth Taylor had been a man she'd have gotten half the denunciations she did. It was a much more patriarchal time."
—Angelina Jolie

"When a man's terrific-looking he's quietly or secretly put down. If he marries, the criticism dies down, like a Rock Hudson, and if he also has kids, like Tyrone Power, it tends to die out. But if a woman's terrific-looking, like Marilyn or Liz or Ava [Gardner] and she doesn't stay married to one man, she's 'wild' and has to be contained and limited."   —actress Nedra Volz (*The Dukes of Hazzard*)

"Blondes connote comedy or romance. Brunettes connote drama or romance. . . . Blonde actresses seldom exert the same dramatic impact. Imagine a blonde playing Medea. They're rather like butterflies—lovely to look at, but not much *gravitas*."
                                                       —ET biographer Sheridan Morley

"It took myriad movies and some decades before Elizabeth Taylor developed a flair for comedy."
—Mark Ricci, coauthor of *The Films of Elizabeth Taylor*

"If you analyze it, all sex symbols are loved and hated. Men lust after them. They also resent them—they're intimidated. More so if the 'girl' is rich, famous, powerful. . . . If she smiles a lot and acts soft, like Marilyn Monroe, there's less flak. If she doesn't smile much and seems rather arrogant, like Liz Taylor, there's more flak."
—Australian author and feminist Germaine Greer

"The public tends to want female stars to be very attractive and very vulnerable. It's the less vulnerable ones who are less liked, more quickly jumped on when they do something that's perceived as wrong. Perfect example: Elizabeth Taylor."   —Natalie Wood

"Women without great looks are judged severely. 'She's a dog.' Women with great looks are judged severely. 'She's a bitch.'"   —Chen Sam, ET's publicist

"I'll tell you what it is: beautiful actresses are considered very lucky, maybe too lucky. They're supposed to have things happen to them. Passive, you know? But Elizabeth Taylor, she made things happen. She was seldom passive."   —comedian Totie Fields

"Elizabeth Taylor had dual British-American citizenship but didn't need a nationality. She was transnational. Her medium was movies and fame itself. Alone or no matter who she was with or what she looked like, what she was doing or wasn't doing, she was always of interest. The public just had to watch her."   —Susan Sarandon

"She had an international impact. What Elizabeth Taylor did mattered. People watched and listened and waited to find out more. Nobody comes close to that nowadays. She was the last genuine VIP superstar."
—Alicia Silverstone

"She had more real-life cliffhangers than anyone. It seemed half the time she was in the hospital or on the verge of dying, and the other half she was in some tempestuous marriage or breaking up somebody else's."
—Francesca Hilton, whose half brother was ET's first husband

"No question she was a naughty girl. Behaved very badly at times. Was sooner or later forgiven. She made life—and Hollywood—less dull."
—actor Ron Glass (*Barney Miller*)

"Elizabeth Taylor . . . I mean wow. Like . . . that was a real movie star."
—Brad Pitt

"I think Elizabeth would be relieved that she's now more remembered as a great star, a fine actress, and a stunning beauty than a homewrecker. For too long she was notorious for supposedly breaking up Eddie Fisher and Debbie Reynolds's family of four and for actually breaking up Sybil and Richard Burton's family of four. But yesterday's headlines become today's historical footnotes."
—costar Rod Taylor (*The V.I.P.s*)

"She definitely had a dark side. What Elizabeth wanted, Elizabeth nearly always got. She was known at different times to use her looks, her stardom, her wealth, etc. That's not to say she was a villain. She was at least as much a heroine and a victim as she was a victimizer."
—Kitty Kelley, author of *Elizabeth Taylor: The Last Star*

"Making *Cleopatra*, after the Liz-and-Dick affair began, when it looked like he would go away with Liz and leave his wife Sybil, Sybil tried to commit suicide. Pills. . . . Ifor, Richard's brother, was there to save Sybil. Then, when it looked like Richard would return to Sybil, Elizabeth tried to commit suicide, to get him to stay. . . . The studio covered it up, said she'd been rushed to the hospital for 'food poisoning.'" —writer Arthur Bell

"Elizabeth Taylor showed Hollywood and the world that a brunette could be as or more beautiful than the blondes that Hollywood movies have been so obsessed with." —Constance Wu (*Fresh Off the Boat*)

"As a raven-haired brunette, I appreciated Elizabeth Taylor's popularity. In the 1950s the studios were going hog-wild for blondes. We were an endangered species. Elizabeth kept ascending through the box-office ranks though actresses were becoming less and less bankable, compared to actors. Ultimately, she transcended categories of hair color and gender and became a singular phenomenon. I still like her." —actress Ruth Roman

"When a third party comes along and a married couple divorces, the third person may unjustifiably be blamed for helping to end a marriage that was practically over anyway." —costar Diana Rigg (*A Little Night Music*)

"The truth about the Eddie Fisher–Debbie Reynolds marriage couldn't be revealed in the 1950s. Eddie Fisher in later decades hinted at the situation. . . . He was more than ready to leave [Reynolds], and—as with any goody-two-shoes-image actress—Debbie wasn't exactly a poor, sweet, innocent, surprised victim." —Jack Kroll, *Newsweek* editor and writer

"It isn't much spotlighted today, but two things that lost Liz Taylor and Marilyn a lot of sympathy back then was the same thing: each married a Jewish man and, to top it off, converted. And Liz had two Jewish husbands. . . . As times have changed, we're not encouraged to mention how very widespread bigotry was, even though it was the anti-democracy McCarthy era."
—columnist Shirley Eder

"It's so great that Elizabeth Taylor chose to become Jewish at a time when that was a very unpopular decision. The lady was fearless."
—Natalie Portman

"I had to give up my title as most beautiful Jewish girl in America when Elizabeth converted. Mind you, that didn't upset me at all."
—Bess Myerson, the first Jewish Miss America

"I know Miss Taylor had two Jewish husbands and she converted [to Judaism]. But I don't agree with the Arab world's boycott of her motion pictures. She is an artist and she should be above political considerations."
—Egyptian-born actor Omar Sharif

"She couldn't go anywhere without a bodyguard,
both for fear of assassination and for the crowds
that began to engulf her whenever she was out in public."
—Kirk Douglas

"It has to be tiresome when you can't go outside and be an individual or one of the crowd. Being Elizabeth Taylor took its toll. Any time she stepped outside her house it was an Appearance, and anything she did was subject to public judgment, often harshly so."
—Hume Cronyn (*Cleopatra*)

"You might be surprised how she looks without the eye makeup. Ladies can cover our hair, change our looks with or without a wig, whatever color. I remember a few times Elizabeth went out in the open and fooled most everybody. She enjoyed that."
—actress and friend Jean Simmons

"When you can't have any kind of a life in a public space that isn't professionally motivated and pre-arranged, it tends to drive you inward. Your emotions become magnified and your indoors life is subject to stress and resentment. This is enough to drive a majority of 'superstars' to drink, or worse. . . . Elizabeth Taylor has survived it pretty well, considering."
—psychologist Dr. Joyce Brothers

"There's the well-known story of Elizabeth in Rome during the months and months of filming *Cleopatra*, yearning for some fresh air and anonymity. So one day she tells her secretary to accompany her, and they drive to a tiny village a few hundred miles away where there's no cinema and few if any TV sets. No one recognizes Elizabeth Taylor. She's free to walk around undisturbed and uninterrupted. No one gawks or whispers or asks for her autograph or smiles in shy embarrassment or acts like she's a goddess descended to earth. That evening, when Dick Burton asks how her excursion went, she sighs. 'Boring . . . awful . . . no one even recognized me.'"
—Carroll O'Connor (*Cleopatra* and TV's *All in the Family*)

"Elizabeth Taylor is a beauty. Just not the most confident beauty. She feels naked without the mascara, eyeliner, and so on. It's part and parcel of her Look. She's said to feel somewhat plain without it." —Kevin McCarthy, actor and close friend of Montgomery Clift

"I once asked if she'd consider modifying how she did her eyes and eyebrows. Nope. Without all that, she isn't Liz Taylor. I thought it looked too raccoon. Especially when she was younger and then when she was older. In between, it didn't look so bad."

—makeup artist Way Bandy

"In person, most stars take you a few seconds to register that it's really them. With her, you know in less than a second. No one else looks like her. Her appearance is so dramatic, and she does sort of take your breath away with what you see and who she is. Elizabeth Taylor has maximum in-person impact."

—producer-director William Castle

"She's so magnetic! When she's on the screen you don't look at anyone else— and it's not so much her looks as it's just *her*. I'd love to have worked with Elizabeth Taylor. Even if she played my mother or something."

—John Travolta

"In the end it's the work that survives. Older people remember the Liz Taylor scandals, but the rest of us, we have only the films . . . so many of them, including so many fascinating or classic ones. It's a hell of a great legacy."

—Lucy Liu

"Yes, the scandals have made her even more popular at the box office. But she didn't set out to engage in a single scandal, and most of them, if she had it to do over again, she would definitely have avoided."

—director George Stevens (*A Place in the Sun, Giant*)

"If the U.S. had royalty, is there any doubt Elizabeth would be our queen? She lives royally. She is known [in the 1960s] for her luggage and entourage, which on a recent trip numbered one-hundred-and-fifty-six suitcases, four children, one governess, three male secretaries, one hairdresser, one nurse, four dogs, a turtle, and two Siamese cats with diamond-studded collars." —columnist Army Archerd

"What she's never had to do is pick up after herself. The first time she ever had to hang her clothes in the closet or anything similar was her first visit to the Betty Ford Center when she was recovering from chemical addiction." —friend and costar Rock Hudson (*Giant*)

"Elizabeth was a good friend, but you didn't really want her for a houseguest. The mess she left behind was nothing compared to the mess her pampered little dogs left behind." —agent and producer Paul Kohner

"Was she alcoholic? During some periods, she was. But Taylor's main substance abuse was through prescribed painkillers. The myriad of accidents and operations she endured . . . she broke her back twice. Without painkillers she'd have dissolved in a puddle of pain." —philanthropist Sybil Brand, who lived to 104

"Alcohol killed Richard Burton, though the official cause was a brain hemorrhage. It did not kill Elizabeth Taylor, who could outdrink her fifth and sixth husband, who were both Richard." —comedian Gary Morton, second husband of Lucille Ball

"It's her desire to live that has pulled her through so many crises in her life. Who knows where that comes from? Maybe it's from actually being at death's door so many times and realizing how precious life is and not wanting to miss out on a second of it. Or it could be a positive outlook at her very core that pushes her onward. Or is it her mother, maybe?"

—ET's hairdresser Jose Eber

"Elizabeth has had pneumonia more times than she can count. Operations on nearly every part of her body. She says she sometimes gets mad at her body because it keeps betraying her. And it doesn't all stem from a horse-riding accident when young. She merely has dramatically bad health—and dramatically good stamina and recuperative powers."
—Brenda Maddox, author of *Who's Afraid of Elizabeth Taylor?*

"That Elizabeth Taylor survived to forty was remarkable. So many times she was expected to die. She even won one Academy Award primarily because she didn't die. . . . Then she made it to fifty, sixty, seventy. She seemed indestructible. She didn't make it to eighty, but talk about the Bionic Woman!"   —Lindsay Wagner (*The Bionic Woman*)

"Elizabeth Taylor's physical decline was sad but slow. It's rather incredible with all the abuse she heaped on herself that she remained beautiful as long as she did. Not to mention that after she got fat—visibly, factually fat—she lost it and came back as beautiful as ever. That woman could do anything—positive and negative."

—author and professor Carolyn G. Heilbrun

"When Elizabeth made her comeback as a world-class beauty, it was through her weight loss, the flattering new black-and-white hairdo, and of course plastic surgery that cut away the excess skin after the fat was gone. She admitted to the first two."

—UK playwright Anthony Shaffer

"Quite apart from being called 'the most beautiful woman in the world,' she just happens to be somebody to whom shocking or tragic things happen . . . a gilt-edged victim. People with humdrum lives like to live vicariously through her." —novelist Jackie Collins

"Some stars with only a fourth of her fame have bigger egos. Elizabeth can be blunt, but she's realistic and occasionally modest. She doesn't believe she's a beauty in the same category as, for instance, Ava Gardner." —costar Lillian Gish (*The Comedians*)

"Elizabeth Taylor isn't mad about her figure. But most men are."

—costar Van Johnson (*The Last Time I Saw Paris*)

"The British admire themselves for being frank or outspoken.
But a friend told me Elizabeth was quite hurt when Richard Burton
publicly catalogued her physical flaws, even though he did it with humor.
He thought he was being admirably candid but it did come across rather cruel.
Wonder how he'd like it if Liz talked about his pockmarked face."
—Evelyn Keyes, actress and an ex-wife of director John Huston
(*The Night of the Iguana*)

"Barbra Streisand and Shirley MacLaine have beautiful hands . . . long fingers and purposefully long fingernails. If you even notice her hands, which I don't think most people do, Elizabeth Taylor rarely paints her fingernails and has shortish fingers. Hands aren't her best feature and she doesn't draw attention to them. When Elizabeth wears a diamond ring she makes sure it's big enough so you notice the ring more than her hand."

—photographer Francesco Scavullo

"Like most female movie stars, Liz is shorter than you think, and her legs are short. . . . It's a peculiar thing about many child stars, female and male, but they grow up, or don't, to be on the short side. Think of Liz, Natalie Wood, Patty Duke, the Harry Potter boy [Daniel Radcliffe], and oh so many others."   —Jackie Cooper, former child star

"The grass is always greener. Elizabeth admires taller, long-waisted women. She herself doesn't have much of a waist. Perhaps she's lucky. As has often been said, a waist is a terrible thing to mind."

—Lynn Redgrave

"In her [motion] pictures, Miss Taylor's bust was not particularly or overly emphasized. Bear in mind that cleavage was for the most part censored. . . . It was in her public dress that she perpetuated a focus on her upper anatomy, with daring and very impressive cleavage. Sometimes with jewelry—a necklace or a pendant—which all but pointed down to the forbidden valley."

—Jeffrey Lettow, entertainment editor of the *Marin Independent Journal*

"The only reason she attracted Mike Todd [Taylor's third husband] was her big breasts, which are overly important to her career."   —rival beauty Marlene Dietrich

"Miss Taylor is a spoiled child and a public disgrace.
The public will soon tire of her."
—Joan Crawford in the 1950s

"Whatever else, Elizabeth Taylor had tact. She kept her criticisms private. She didn't do the older-actress thing of publicly disparaging younger actresses. That happened a lot when Marilyn Monroe came along—so many established female stars took a crack at Marilyn."   —Jeanne Martin, ex-wife of Dean

"Elizabeth knew firsthand what it was like to be put down in public. Repeatedly. I don't think she cared to visit that upon other people, unless they were truly abhorrent to her."
—Roddy McDowall, friend and costar (*Lassie, Come Home*)

"The press was fairly openly anti-Jewish in those days, and when Elizabeth Taylor converted to Judaism for the man she loved [Eddie Fisher], she was more or less openly criticized everywhere but in Hollywood."   —talk show host Virginia Graham

"Elizabeth thought of converting during her marriage to Mike [Todd]. He resisted it. When she talked about it to me, I resisted it, knowing how much anti-Semitism there is out there. I didn't want her to suffer. But she was determined, and her studies were something we did together. I hadn't known as much about my religious or cultural background until I studied it with Elizabeth."   —fourth husband Eddie Fisher

"She was actually criticized for replacing Vivien Leigh in *Elephant Walk*. Leigh was having mental problems, so Liz was brought in as leading lady. Not her fault, but the Hollywood press didn't want actresses to get swelled heads. . . . Any divorce that Liz experienced, including the first, from the no-good Hilton, she was often blamed for it!"
—Marni Nixon, singing voice–double for Audrey Hepburn,
Deborah Kerr, and Natalie Wood

"I recently told a friend's niece about the outcry when Elizabeth Taylor was paid a million dollars to star as Cleopatra. She couldn't believe it. 'So little?' She's also too young to remember when Barbara Walters was the first news anchor to be paid a million a year. Because that was more than any man was being paid, public indignation ran high. No news anchor is worth that much, many people said. What they meant was, no woman is worth that much. You have to look back and realize."   —actress Jean Byron (*Dobie Gillis*)

"It's always noted that Liz Taylor got a mil for *Cleopatra*
and was the first to do so. But she got substantially more than that,
due to her contract's clauses about all the over-time."
—Julia Phillips, producer (*The Sting*)

"When Elizabeth Taylor was paid one million dollars for *Cleopatra* much of the public and part of Hollywood was outraged. No one had ever been paid that for one picture. It was considered obscenely greedy and a regrettable fluke. But within a few years Marlon Brando and Audrey Hepburn were also getting a million, and from there on things went up, or down, depending on your viewpoint."
—two-time Oscar winner and Member of Parliament Glenda Jackson

"When you look back at the ads and posters announcing *Cleopatra*, it was so blatant—especially for that era—how prominently they zoomed in on, or center-staged, Elizabeth Taylor's breasts and cleavage."　　　　　—Madeline Kahn (*What's Up, Doc?*)

"I was forced to threaten lawsuit when pictorial advertising for *Cleopatra* omitted myself as Julius Caesar. . . . Rather than all three principals, only 'Liz and Dick' were pictured, thanks to their much bruited-about relationship. . . . Of course my image was restored . . . and jocularly referred to as 'great Caesar's ghost.'"　　　　　—Rex Harrison

"When a movie is super-expensive and stars a major actress and isn't a runaway hit, the media prefers to call it a non-hit or even a flop. Contrary to box-office figures. It happened with several Joan Crawford movies and with *Cleopatra* and *Hello, Dolly!* [starring Barbra Streisand]. Those movies were financial hits. But when a film's budget is extremely high, it would have to be a *Sound of Music*–type earner to be considered a big hit."　　　　　—Harry Walders, film distributor

"A prominent factor in the cost overruns and delays on *Cleopatra* was Elizabeth Taylor's poor health. Some was due to her mental condition, specifically, her volatile relationship with Richard Burton. She didn't callously steal him from his wife. She did feel remorse and personal conflict. And he didn't fall head over heels for Liz. He too was torn, but Richard was ambitious and aware that Elizabeth Taylor was his gateway from stardom to superstardom."
—ET's secretary Roger Wall

"What was never mentioned in the time of Marilyn Monroe and Liz Taylor, or hardly ever today, is that some actresses have a terrible, painful time with their periods. That can exacerbate existing health conditions, if any. . . . The on-set delays or absences which that caused were nobody's fault. Despite that, the press frequently called these highly-paid women spoiled or 'difficult.'"   —journalist Shana Alexander

"It's scandalous how much less Marilyn Monroe was paid per film than Taylor. At the time they were making concurrent movies, Marilyn was earning a tenth of what Elizabeth got . . . until Fox re-hired her after the famous firing and renegotiated her contract. . . . The moguls thought of blondes as even less respectable than brunette actresses, as bimbos instead of semi talents." —Sybil Brand, widow of Fox publicist Harry Brand

"A big reason Marilyn posed semi-nude in the swimming pool scene [in her uncompleted film *Something's Got to Give*] was an attempt to knock Liz Taylor and *Cleopatra* off the magazine covers. The movie-magazine coverage was Liz, Liz, Liz or Liz and Dick, Liz and Dick. It worked. Marilyn Monroe al fresco in the nighttime pool made magazine covers worldwide. She was as beautiful as ever, but then tragedy had to strike and take her away several weeks later, at 36."   —Dean Martin, Marilyn Monroe's final costar

"How I would love to know what Elizabeth Taylor really felt when Marilyn Monroe died. A topic I don't believe she ever spoke about publicly. And if she spoke about it privately, no one who heard has ever said."   —cable-TV talk show host Skip E. Lowe

"Elizabeth was jealous of Marilyn's beauty—she felt she coasted on it. Marilyn was jealous of the meaty roles Elizabeth got and of her growing acclaim. . . . Each had a celebrated private life that wasn't very private. They were, in essence, competing goddesses."

—Paula Dell, stuntwoman and acrobat

"Marilyn was more jealous of Taylor's career, while Taylor was more jealous of Marilyn herself. But at one point Elizabeth called her 'that dyke.' Norman Mailer put that in his book on Marilyn and Taylor was going to sue but backed off because apparently he had proof of the comment."

—writer E. Lynn Harris

"Most stars crave peace and calm in their private lives. There's enough hubbub in their professional lives. But some are true drama queens, male or female. Friends of Liz Taylor say she bores easily and needs a drama a day. She loves to laugh and she loves to gossip and she loves to love."

—Hollywood business manager Morgan Maree

"With Elizabeth there was no such thing as normal life. The only thing predictable about our life was that it would be chaos. With Elizabeth, something was always happening, and if it wasn't, she made it happen. If nothing was happening, she would start a fight. Every day was a surprise."

—Eddie Fisher

"Elizabeth has endured personal tragedies and scandals that would send half of Hollywood to their psychiatrists on a daily basis. It's interesting that she's one of few stars who has never visited a shrink."

—ET's publicist Chen Sam

"Some of the scandal sheets say my daughter has caused others to suffer. All I can say is she has a huge heart. She is very loving and she loves being in love. . . . Any suffering she ever caused, she herself has suffered that much more."

—mother Sara Taylor (nee Warmbrodt)

"Most child stars don't make it to adult stardom. Most that do are female, like Liz Taylor and Natalie Wood. Both of those had fierce stage mothers. Taylor's mother was a failed actress and rather a desperate woman. Once, at least, she slept with a producer to get her daughter a good role."   —Gore Vidal, who cowrote ET's movie *Suddenly, Last Summer*

"Sara was always socially ambitious, more so after she stopped being a moderately successful stage actress named Sara Sothern. She had very dark hair like Elizabeth but eventually went blonde so she wouldn't detract from her daughter's snow-white face and jet-black hair. For a long time, everywhere Elizabeth went, Sara went."

—columnist Joyce Haber

"Elizabeth was very devoted to her mother, who lived to be very elderly [ninety-nine]. And she was *absolutely* devoted to her father."
—Kate Burton, Richard's actress daughter

"In 1946 there was a press item about Elizabeth Taylor's parents separating. But Elizabeth's potential was evident—she'd already done *National Velvet*. The mother fought to keep the marriage intact, at least outwardly so, for the sake of [ET's] career. Rumors persisted that Sara had blackmailed Francis out of seeking a divorce."

—columnist Sheilah Graham

"In England, Sara was always what is now called networking. Early on, she introduced her husband to a handsome 38-year-old bachelor politician named Victor Cazalet. It was love at first sight; the men became lovers, and Cazalet helped Sara's family financially and in high society. As an art collector he was able to enhance Francis Taylor's art gallery business."   —ET biographer David Bret

"During the filming of *Father of the Bride*, Francis Taylor had an affair with its director, Vicente Minnelli, the former husband of Judy Garland."   —ET's secretary Roger Wall

"As an actress, Elizabeth took good care of her parents financially
but her father retreated further into himself and the bottle,
overwhelmed and perhaps trapped as he was by the domineering,
enervating Sara and the skyrocketing Liz."
—actor Kevin McCarthy (*Invasion of the Body Snatchers*)

"Francis Taylor had a serious stroke three years before his death. After he died Elizabeth felt very guilty over not having been closer to him during her busy adult years. . . . He lived to about seventy. Elizabeth then drew closer to her mother, but after Sara passed seventy, eighty, ninety, and so forth, they were close but not that close. There was always some mother-daughter friction."   —British director Bryan Forbes

"Elizabeth's father died yesterday afternoon and I had to break the news to her. She was like a wild animal even though we've been expecting his death for some years."
—from Richard Burton's diary entry for November 21, 1968

"A young actor recently [in 2001] asked Elizabeth Taylor her advice on coming out of the closet. She said, 'I'd say come out. And embrace those you love and that love you.' Excellent advice. But alas more so for a non-actor."
—producer Daniel Melnick (*Making Love*)

"Of course Taylor is a gay icon, known for her close friendships with gay and bisexual actors like Monty Clift, Rock Hudson, James Dean, Roddy McDowall, Laurence Harvey, etc. But it goes back further than that, since her father was gay. As was Judy Garland's. Both their fathers died prematurely and both were deeply missed by their daughters. However, Liz stuck by her mother, while Judy detested hers—called her 'the real Wicked Witch of the West.'"
—columnist Lee Graham

"Like so many actresses whose careers were fostered by their mothers, Elizabeth's relationship with hers grew prickly. Such mothers don't want to cut the gilded umbilical cord . . . daughters eventually resent the control. It's usual in such situations for the daughter to honor the mother, fiscally, but to widen their distance. Particularly once her love life takes precedence."
—actress Rachel Kempson, widow of Michael Redgrave and mother of Vanessa

"The consensus is that Elizabeth didn't want Sara to be all that close to Elizabeth's children. Sara tended to give orders rather than affection. She was a disciplinarian, where Elizabeth was more easygoing with her children and had no intention of bringing them into the business. She wanted them to have basically normal and pleasant childhoods."
—British star and friend Jean Simmons

"How normal a childhood did Elizabeth Taylor have? Her ruling parent was MGM. In 1949 the studio picked and assigned a tall blond UCLA athlete named Bob Precht to take Elizabeth to her school prom. They made a very photogenic impression."

—former child star Roddy McDowall

"Elizabeth failed to apply discipline or limits. Her two sons were spoiled rotten, hell-raisers as boys and teens. It's a wonder they turned out fairly okay."

—press agent Bill Feeder

"One thing Elizabeth drummed into her kids was to live their own lives but avoid scandal. She definitely controls the purse strings; whether she's used that to keep her kids in line I don't know. But none has made headlines or embarrassed her, and you can bet the media was just waiting for something like that to happen."   —costar Dina Merrill (*Butterfield 8*)

"Some children of actors try or dabble in acting, but none of Elizabeth Taylor's four children became famous. That speaks well for her as a mother."
—Ricardo Montalban, none of whose offspring became famous either

"A famous and stupidly bigoted actor once asked Elizabeth if she worried about her boys being around some of her gay actor friends. Without losing her temper she said no more than she worried about her girls being around some of her straight actor friends. Elizabeth didn't have a big intellect, but she had common sense."

—actor Jack Larson (Jimmy Olsen on TV's *Superman*)

"Elizabeth has always been a loyal friend. After Montgomery Clift was no longer insurable to star in a movie, she offered the producers her big salary as a guarantee and a possible forfeit for him. Clift badly needed a comeback and she was the only one with the power and the generosity to make it possible."
—Tennessee Williams

"Monty would have been brilliant as her gay husband [in *Reflections in a Golden Eye*]. Unfortunately, he died before filming began. Richard [Burton, Taylor's then-husband] had had a homosexual relationship when he was young, a fact he didn't hide. But he didn't want to play the gay husband. So they went and got Brando."
—costar Shelley Winters (*A Place in the Sun*)

"She's usually billed first. It's a habit or custom of long-standing. I think most of us, the men, we don't mind much. I, for one, did not haggle over billing. She's just first-billed . . . that's that."
—Marlon Brando

"When we made *National Velvet* Liz was 12, I think, and I remember thinking someday she might possibly be a star. But that was my picture. I never imagined she'd steal it out from under me. Which she did. Not that I hold a grudge. That movie's super-famous now . . . thanks to her."
—Mickey Rooney

"I knew going in that this sequel wouldn't compare and that I was no Elizabeth Taylor. But, like, who is?"
—Tatum O'Neal, about the flop *International Velvet*

"I loved how Elizabeth Taylor's character fell in love with her horse . . . how they bonded and she defied society and its taboos. I could really identify with that. I'm sure thousands of girls did, and do."
—Keira Knightley

"As a child actress Elizabeth did movies with horses and dogs. . . . She loved animals and was more comfortable around them than people, who could turn on her. She never blamed the horse that threw her and started her back problems and years of physical misery."
—costar Elsa Lanchester (*Lassie, Come Home*)

"Elizabeth always liked animals . . . one reason is they were gentle and didn't speak up. As a very young star she didn't speak up for herself. She only learned to speak up when she heard Louis B. Mayer at Metro [MGM] shouting abuse at our mother. Elizabeth immediately defended her and for the first time felt a sense of her own power."
—brother Howard Taylor

"The focus has always been on Elizabeth Taylor's looks. But that's not the whole picture. Early on, she had a chipmunk named Nibbles that was her favorite pet. After *National Velvet* she was asked to do a book about him . . . Elizabeth illustrated the book too. That's some kid!"
—George Cukor, who directed ET in *The Blue Bird*

"*Nibbles and Me* [1946] is a darling book and a classic of its kind. Have you seen it? And she did all the illustrations, some in green, some beige. Elizabeth's talent floored me. She could easily have gone on to be a children's-book author and illustrator."
—Gretchen Wyler, actress and animal-rights activist

"If she'd stayed in England, where she was born [to American parents], Elizabeth Taylor would probably have become a debutante—belle of the ball—then married well and lived happily ever after. Or not so happily. Maybe even divorced."
—British actor Stewart Granger, husband of Jean Simmons

"Elizabeth always enjoyed shopping. But came a time her fame grew so, she couldn't enter a shop without drawing a crowd within several minutes. So she had to have clothes sent to her home or hotel to choose from. That maintained her privacy but did away with the pleasure of going out and spending hours window-shopping or exploring boutiques and department stores."
—ET's secretary Dick Hanley

"One has to wonder who selects Elizabeth Taylor's public costumes. For, costumes they are, with an unwavering emphasis on cleavage that contradicts the Oscar winner's stated self-description as a dramatic actress."
—Hebe Dorsey, fashion editor of the *International Herald Tribune*

"All my life I wanted to look like Elizabeth Taylor . . . now I find she's beginning to look like me."
—obese female impersonator Divine

"Oh, Elizabeth Taylor!! I tried to take her to McDonald's but she wouldn't fit through the golden arches! She has more Chins than a Chinese phone book. Yes!! . . . It's not mean if it's true."
—Joan Rivers

"Like maybe there came a time after the two divorces from Dick Burton and all those movies that she just decided, Hey, I'll eat whatever I enjoy and push all that maintenance and time and effort holding onto my looks onto the back burner. And to hell with what anybody thinks. So Elizabeth Taylor got fat. Big f---ing crime."　　　　—Roseanne Barr

"While she was heavy, Elizabeth said she was perfectly happy. After she lost the weight she admitted the fat had been the result of unhappiness. Her relationship with the right-wing politician [John Warner] was not a happy one, as she revealed post-marriage."
　　　　　　　—talk show host Phil Donahue

"At lunch, Elizabeth said to me that one piece of chocolate is wonderful, and two might be. Three is okay. But more than four or five is unhealthy and unsatisfying—and psychological."
—five-time Oscar-winning costume designer Irene Sharaff

"The way she was able to go back from being fat to being so beautiful is an absolute inspiration and proves that it can be done. I mean to lose the fat, not necessarily to become so beautiful."　　　　—actress Kathy Najimy

"I heard that the cover photo of [the book] *Hollywood Babylon II* showing Liz Taylor emerging from a car looking like a lavender mountain carrying a purse was a deciding factor in her choosing to lose weight. Everyone was commenting about that awful picture. I don't know if Liz stuck that picture on her fridge, but I've read Maria Callas the fat opera singer stuck a picture of skinny Audrey Hepburn on her fridge until she finally lost the weight. Whatever it takes. . . ."　　　　—Dixie Carter (*Designing Women*)

"As a child she was sweet and pretty as a picture. When I played the title role in *Jane Eyre*, Elizabeth Taylor had a bit as a little girl in the childhood sequence. Her looks and coloring, like Snow White, made her stand out. But I couldn't foresee that when we would make another film a slight eight years later [in 1952] she would have progressed so far professionally and matrimonially. And that was only the beginning!"

—Joan Fontaine

"In *Sunset Boulevard* Gloria Swanson says, 'We had faces then,' about past stars, compared to mere types—or clones. In the 1950s we had variety then. The top four female stars were distinctly separate, each uniquely wonderful: Audrey Hepburn, Marilyn Monroe, Elizabeth Taylor, Doris Day. Is there anything remotely comparable today?"

—actress-director Ida Lupino

"The most publicized movies ever are still *Gone with the Wind* and *Cleopatra*. An often overlooked fact is that the latter was supposed to star myself as Mark Anthony, Peter Finch as Julius Caesar, and Joan Collins as Cleopatra. . . . . Liz got the title role. It began filming in England . . . a ton of money was spent. Then came mystery, delays, studio politics, excuses . . . and Miss Taylor's illnesses. *Cleopatra* was redesigned, rescripted, relocated to Rome with new male costars—and the rest is history."

—Stephen Boyd (*Ben-Hur*)

"Elizabeth Taylor looks like two small boys fighting under a mink blanket."
—fashion designer Mr. Blackwell of the annual Ten Worst-Dressed Women list

"For its interminable shooting period, *Cleopatra* was the most publicized film, and scandal, ever. By comparison, *Gone with the Wind* was shot overnight. Also, the actual shooting of GWTW wasn't heavily publicized. And if anybody was committing adultery during its making, you bet it wasn't publicized. Unlike *Cleopatra*!"

—columnist Lloyd Shearer

"I'd already played Egyptian in *Land of the Pharaohs* [1955]. . . . Peter Finch would have made a marvelous Julius Caesar–Rex Harrison [in the 1963 Taylor version] was a little old for the part. I'm not as sure about Stephen Boyd."

—Joan Collins

"There was an earlier set of [*Cleopatra*] costumes . . . and had photographs of Liz Taylor wearing some of them been released to the public there would have been controversy and threatened boycotts. In one of them, more than half of her breasts are exposed, with a gold string holding up one of two white patches. Such a costume probably couldn't have been used on screen anyway."

—costume designer Ray Aghayan

"Taylor asked for a cool million dollars when producer Walter Wanger offered her the role, which she wasn't keen on. She didn't believe anyone would pay that amount. Wanger said he'd get back to her. When he did, he said Fox wanted Susan Hayward to play Cleopatra. By that time, Liz coveted the role. More so, when she heard they wanted Hayward. Liz was ready to settle for $750,000 and ten percent of the gross, also numerous perks. Whatever she actually earned for the picture, when she and Fisher divorced the settlement figure agreed upon for *Cleopatra* was said to be $7 million."

—Hollywood business manager Morgan Maree

"In Richard Burton, her fifth husband, Elizabeth finally found a prince consort, someone with enough looks, charm, wit, and charisma to last her . . . for quite a while. Eventually he complained that she was 'more famous than the Queen,' but added that he would love her until he died. Richard was often unhappy with Elizabeth, but that was his personality. Without her, he was hardly ever happy. Whatever else, they shared a tremendous passion."
—movie writer Jane Ardmore

"All told, Liz and Dick were in eleven movies together. One was just a Taylor cameo in a Burton feature [*Anne of the Thousand Days*]. Their last was just a TV movie, an indication of how far they'd fallen box-office-wise by 1973. At least it was reportedly the most expensive TV movie ever made—a last hurrah for the most famous couple in Hollywood history."
—film critic Robin Wood

"The public loved seeing Elizabeth Taylor and Richard Burton on screen together because it let them in close-up on the love affair of the century. Naturally, with the passing of time and, truth to tell, some idiotic choices on the couple's part, the attraction waned. New faces are always coming along, and the public is nothing if not fickle."
—British actor Trevor Howard

"I remember thinking how masochistic it was of Richard and Elizabeth to insert themselves into this very personal story of divorce when it was clear to most everyone around them that divorce was looming large on their horizon."
—actress-director Ida Lupino

"Prophetically, the final Taylor-Burton collaboration was *Divorce His/Divorce Hers*. It had two halves, each with a different viewpoint and justification. It did well in the ratings. Guess why . . . people wanted to believe it was more documentary than fiction. By then it was common knowledge that the lovebirds who'd sacrificed so much and undergone so much opprobrium were arguing as much, or more, than they weren't."

—British actress Coral Browne

"*Divorce His* and *Divorce Hers*—too long of a gimmicky, over-produced telefilm, and sheer self-exploitation. It's Taylor-Burton-made for voyeurs by exhibitionists."

—film critic Wyatt Cooper (Anderson's father)

"Since they were having gargantuan, often public, marital squabbles, I guess Liz and Dick figured they might as well put it all up on the screen and get paid for it. . . . Despite their protestations, Liz and Dick reveled in publicity and high drama—and were often high doing it!"

—Truman Capote

"At least after watching Liz and Dick agonize at length on television whether or not to get a divorce, when the real thing happens no one will have to be shocked. Between this 'prestige' small-screen offering and what one reads in the fanzines and even newspapers, one may wonder why it took so long."

—Hollywood agent Ann Dollard

"Jacqueline Kennedy came in for almost as much criticism for simply remarrying as Elizabeth Taylor did for divorcing and re-divorcing, etc. Elizabeth and Richard were rooting for her when she married Onassis. They didn't like him much—a rich, greasy publicity hound with no looks or class. But they felt Jackie had a right to pursue her own life. Whereas the Establishment expected Jackie, after President Kennedy's assassination, to wear widow's weeds until her death."   —Truman Capote

"After Marilyn died, Elizabeth and Jackie were the most famous women of the 1960s. Elizabeth was almost eclipsed by Jackie Kennedy when she married Aristotle Onassis, the Greek tycoon. For over a decade, it was Liz or Jackie, and sometimes both, on magazine covers, regularly."   —Andy Warhol, whose portrait of ET hung in her living room

"Onassis married Jackie Kennedy to what appears to be the general disapproval of the USA. . . . We shall send them a telegram of congratulations today. Dick Hanley [ET's secretary] says Jackie will be declared a 'public sinner.' In a comical world the Vatican is sometimes the most comical thing in it. I remember some years ago that [they] recommended that Elizabeth was an unfit mother for her children and that they should be forcibly removed from her! Silly pompous asses."   —from Richard Burton's diary entry for October 21, 1968

CHAPTER 2

The Actress

"Elizabeth doesn't claim to be the most versatile actress, she's not a Meryl Streep, but she invests her roles with passion. She makes them more exciting than they appear on paper or might be through another actress."

—Robert Wagner, friend and costar (*There Must Be a Pony*)

"As a child star she was decorative and sometimes intense. As an adult star she cannot help dominating every scene and every performer. She is like the eye at the center of the storm—and she is also the storm."

—French actress Marion Cotillard

"When you look like Elizabeth Taylor you know movie stardom is in store. Not to mention her above-it-all demeanor. Others of us had to struggle to be taken seriously as movie actors and stars. Nature just slotted her into that category."

—Sally Field

"In her movies she's often breaking the rules. Taylor's characters, like her, aren't passive. They're not content. They want something else. They want *more*."

—fashion designer Isaac Mizrahi

"I titled my book about Elizabeth Taylor *The Accidental Feminist* because my thesis is that she and her screen characters raised our consciousness but we were too distracted by her beauty to notice."
                                                                  —cultural historian M. G. Lord

"People today can just watch Liz Taylor's films and be entertained or moved and judge her as an actor. During her heyday, much of the public didn't or wouldn't watch her films objectively . . . some were boycotting her films or watching and judging her as this scandalous, spoiled woman."
                                        —Betty White

"Her life and image interfered with the perception of what she delivered as a performer."
                                                                  —Maggie Gyllenhaal

"Cleopatra wanted to rule her world, an impossible dream. Martha [in *Who's Afraid of Virginia Woolf?*] wanted a perfect marriage—there's no such thing. Et cetera and so forth. It's riveting to watch Elizabeth *want*. Most of her characters cannot make their dreams come true, but oh, how Elizabeth makes them try."
                        —friend and costar Laurence Harvey (*Butterfield 8* and *Night Watch*)

"*Who's Afraid of Virginia Woolf?* is usually cited as the film most responsible for ending unrealistic Hollywood screen censorship. The words in it made it adults-only viewing in 1966 but that's how people talked, and it's totally tame by today's foul-mouthed standards."
                                                        —Australian actor Hugh Jackman

"We had no nudity, just off-screen adultery. There was language, but nothing, uh, scorching. But what Elizabeth Taylor said and did on-screen, that just . . . it simply . . . it blew away the hypocrisy and censorship of the movie ratings system."

—*Woolf* costar and Oscar-winner Sandy Dennis

"Elizabeth Taylor is not the most beautiful actress, which that would be an opinion and what does it matter? She *is* one of the most interesting actors or actresses. *That* matters."

—French actress Isabelle Huppert

"She is one of very few stars who regardless of a given film's quality, it's worth watching for *her*. When she first comes on the screen, it's what you've been waiting for. She holds your attention, quietly—until she breaks out emotionally. If it's a lousy movie and Elizabeth is in it from the first scene, you only gradually notice that it's a lousy movie."

—Robert Vaughn (*The Man from U.N.C.L.E.*)

"Ironically, her first Oscar was for a film she abhorred [*Butterfield 8*], enacting a high-class call girl. She tried everything to avoid doing it, but she owed MGM one more project before she was contractually free of them. After completing it she publicly declared, 'This picture stinks.' Most of the critics agreed. Her peers handed her an Oscar for it. In reality it was for her [previously Oscar-nominated] work in *Suddenly, Last Summer* and because she nearly died after completing *Butterfield 8*. Nor did it hurt that her character in the film died."

—Richard Burton

"I lost to a goddamn tracheotomy!"
—simultaneously Oscar-nominated Shirley MacLaine

"Taylor took lots of time off when Mike Todd produced and promoted *Around the World in Eighty Days*. He wanted to make a great event of a movie. It was based on Jules Verne's novel and had dozens of big stars in tiny roles. The leads were Britisher David Niven, Mexican Cantinflas, and Shirley MacLaine as a Hindu princess. It was a great hit and won the Oscar for Best Picture of 1956."　　　　　—writer Boyd McDonald

"In the 1950s Mike Todd planned a movie about the maestro Arturo Toscanini. It came to nothing, but Todd, a huckster and a vulgarian, was always chasing class and validation. Elizabeth Taylor met Toscanini in the '50s . . . three decades later she had a role in *Young Toscanini* as a diva—a soprano. While dubbed, she 'performed' an aria from the opera *Aida*. When Elizabeth first heard the name, she asked, 'Who's Aida?'"
　　　　　—actor Ron Vawter (*Silence of the Lambs*)

"Like Howard Hughes, Todd wanted to be an A-list moviemaker . . . neither had the prerequisites to direct, they were deal-makers. . . . Elizabeth was never considered to star [in *Around the World in Eighty Days*]. Todd wanted a just-camp-enough actress—pretty but not beautiful, fey but not comical. . . . When Shirley MacLaine auditioned I saw the campy quality and told Mike and he hired her."
　　　　　—Dick Hanley, Mike Todd's executive secretary

"Mike inherited secretary Dick Hanley from Louis B. Mayer, who sacked him after more than ten years of faithful service. When Mike died, Elizabeth made him her personal secretary. Dick became her right arm. He was gay, so there was no funny business . . . because the moment the press saw a man next to Elizabeth they automatically assumed an affair or cheating."　　　　　—Eddie Fisher

"By age eighteen Elizabeth had embarked on the marital career that would seriously compete with her movie career. Each fed the other, both fed her self-engorging fame."
—actor George Sanders, once married to Zsa Zsa Gabor, who was once married to Conrad Hilton, whose son Nicholas was ET's first husband

"Elizabeth Taylor's mother had been thrilled to play Broadway but when she married in 1926 she retired. She and her husband Francis didn't have a child until 1929, a son, and then a daughter in 1932. Sara's greatest success was her daughter's superstardom. . . . She left behind an unpublished manuscript titled *Taylor-made Memories*."

—novelist Jackie Collins

"How talented is Elizabeth Taylor? The question is irrelevant. Movies are for audiences. They're not talent shows."   —producer George Jessel

"*Giant* made Elizabeth a megastar and proved she could act. Every name actress in Hollywood had been campaigning for the role, which now seems so clearly tailor-made for her. . . . At one point, [director] George Stevens asked leading man Rock Hudson whom he preferred for his leading lady, Grace Kelly or Elizabeth Taylor? Having met Elizabeth through Monty Clift and knowing she was simpatico with gays, he replied, 'Elizabeth Taylor,' and Stevens said, 'Fine, we'll get Elizabeth.'"

—ET biographer Ellis Amburn

"Miss Taylor is a very good actress within her range. However, her range is not very wide."   —film critic Wyatt Cooper

"The voice limits her. It's too high-pitched too often, with a tendency toward childish petulance or near-hysteria. . . . After *Virginia Woolf* she was increasingly cast as nagging wives and harpies. Her eyes went wider too often and her voice too often became a shrill demand or a challenge to the leading man. Repetition did her in."

—ex–casting director Renée Valente

"After the '60s star actresses weren't big box office, with the possible exception of la Streisand. And you knew Liz wasn't going to take supporting roles, not for some time. . . . She longed to do another Tennessee Williams character, to revive her old successes. Her mistake was doing it [*Sweet Bird of Youth*] as a TV movie—a real comedown—and doing it opposite not a Paul Newman, like in the motion picture, but one Mark Harmon. She recreated, not very well, a role brilliantly performed, to Oscar-nominated acclaim, by Geraldine Page in the movie. People still remembered her and the movie. Liz even tinted her hair red, a bad move because Page's hair was red in the movie."

—comedian and acting coach Charles Nelson Reilly

"The three phases of Liz, three stereotypes: the nice-girl child star, the voluptuous, strong-willed beauty, the shrew."
—columnist James Bacon

"What ever possessed her to go on-screen in [Agatha Christie's] *The Mirror Crack'd* looking, or weighing, as she did? The other female lead was Kim Novak—she looked svelte and fantastic. In one scene where they pose for photos Kim's character tells her, 'Chin up, sweetie. Both of them.' That has to have hurt. Yet Liz had no one to blame but herself."

—Peg Bracken, author of *The I Hate to Cook Cookbook*

"Elizabeth and I reunited in *The Mirror Crack'd*. It was great fun. It was a joy to be working together again. *Giant* seemed like a lifetime ago. . . . What I did resent were movie critics' barbs about her weight. It in no way detracted from the picture."

—Rock Hudson

"Christie based her story on a real-life event. Movie star Gene Tierney, best known for *Laura*, was hugged and kissed at the Hollywood Canteen by a devoted female fan in the Armed Forces who should have remained in quarantine but instead passed on German measles to the pregnant actress. As a result, Tierney's daughter was born mentally retarded . . . Tierney had subsequent mental problems and was temporarily institutionalized."

—columnist Radie Harris

"Sooner or later, most top female stars wind up playing themselves. Which is what's happened in *The Mirror Crack'd* with Elizabeth Taylor, except that she turns out to be the murderess. Otherwise, she's a faded, overfed American movie star playing a faded, overfed American movie star."

—Christopher Price, BBC host and journalist

"Elizabeth is an instinctual actress. She hasn't had lessons . . . she *feels* what is required in a scene. We discussed this on location in Russia, where the Method and all that nonsense originated. Elizabeth concurs that an actor is not supposed to try to be interesting, an actor is supposed to be convincing. Elizabeth is innately interesting and she is convincing. It's the script that's supposed to be interesting. A good script and good actors—a good movie. Bad script, good actors—a waste-of-time movie."

—director George Cukor

"I think it in deplorable taste for Miss Taylor to portray a character clearly suggested by my former wife and a tragic, much-publicized situation in this film of a popular novel."
—Gene Tierney's ex-husband, designer Oleg Cassini

"In *The Blue Bird*, a 1976 remake of a Shirley Temple movie, Elizabeth played a mother, a witch, and some sort of good fairy. In smaller parts, Ava Gardner and Jane Fonda, but . . . such a mish-mash. It was the first Russian-American co-production and I believe the last. The sheer incompetence! The horrors of the Russian location . . . and it dragged on and on. Not for me, thank you—I had a distinctly minor role. Russian crews? The worst. Work ethic? No work ethic."
—Sir Robert Morley

"Dear old George Cukor pleased the Russians when he declared himself proud to be working in the same studio as Sergei Eisenstein—both directors were gay and Jewish. He had filmed *Battleship Potemkin* there in 1925. The interpreter beamed and said, 'Yes, Mr. Cukor, and with much of the very same equipment we are using now.'"
—ET biographer Sheridan Morley (Robert's son)

"Elizabeth didn't settle for being labeled just sexy or a movie star. She had acting ambitions. . . . After her first time working with Montgomery Clift [in *A Place in the Sun*] she sought out acting challenges. His work had majorly impressed her, but her mother feared if she went to the Actors Studio for lessons she'd become a laughingstock, which later happened to Marilyn Monroe."
—Susan Strasberg, daughter of Actors Studio head Lee Strasberg

"Monty privately tutored Elizabeth. . . . For the most part she stuck to what she knew. Sometimes you don't want to tamper with what makes you tick. Too much self-knowledge inhibits some actors. If you're not Method-oriented, as I am, it's probably best just to go with the flow."   —Shelley Winters, winner of two supporting Oscars

"People always talked about how Taylor 'ruined' Burton's career, how he went from a talent to a golden hack. Yet it worked both ways. As a team they worked for the biggest bucks, and after they stopped teaming—by public demand!— Taylor opted for prestigious writers and directors regardless how static the screenplay or inappropriate her part. By then she just wanted to stay on top." —James Card, film preservationist

"Elizabeth knew someday she would want and have to do theatre. In those days Broadway was the acme of acting. Almost every movie actor had some stage background. She didn't. . . . Elizabeth eventually acted in two plays and formed her own theatrical company. I admire the determination and effort. After her awards for movie acting she could have but didn't sit on her laurels."   —talk show host Virginia Graham

"My wife Anne [Jackson] said Elizabeth always admired and envied businesswomen like Lucille Ball or Gloria Swanson, who made a fortune designing clothes and dress patterns. . . . Elizabeth was very sensual and loved beautiful scents. She jumped in head first when it came time to create and promote her signature fragrance, Passion. . . . Ultimately, Elizabeth Taylor made more money from her line of perfumes than her acting career." —costar Eli Wallach (*Winter Kills*)

"In 1987, in the midst of her AIDS work, she licensed her name to the perfumes division of Chesebrough-Pond and debuted her own personal fragrance, Elizabeth Taylor's Passion. Later there would be White Diamonds, Passion for Men, Violet Eyes . . . also The House of Taylor, her own jewelry company. Chesebrough-Pond invested over $10 million in Elizabeth's perfume, and she crossed the country promoting it. It became an enormous success."
—publicist Andrea Jaffe

"The print and TV ads for Elizabeth Taylor's Passion were beautifully done, and by 1990 it was the country's fourth-most-popular women's perfume, grossing over $70 million a year. By then Elizabeth was worth $100 million, mostly thanks to her perfume business."
—costume designer Arnold Scaasi (Isaacs, spelled backward)

"When she hit it big with scents, several people advised Elizabeth to backpedal on her battle against AIDS and settle into being a glamorous icon and businesswoman. She refused. She stepped up her activism and used her renewed public profile with the perfumes to raise more money for AIDS research."
—Bette Midler

"In *Giant*, set in Texas, Elizabeth Taylor's character is the movie's conscience. Basically, the U.S. stole Texas from Mexico, and Taylor's character confronts the Anglos who discriminate against Mexicans and Mexican-Americans. That film, from 1956, still holds up today."
—Edward James Olmos

"In *Suddenly, Last Summer* she's pitted against Katharine Hepburn as an old prude who wants Liz lobotomized for admitting that Hepburn's late son was gay. . . . In *The Sandpiper* she's independent, a Pagan-spirited, freethinking artist local churchgoers want to run out of town. . . . During the first half or two-thirds of her movie career Elizabeth Taylor's characters were usually more natural and free, more progressive, than the rest."
—film historian Carlos Clarens

"One thing I like about her and her movies is Elizabeth Taylor basically always rebels in them. Against authority or restrictions. And she was a rebel—with a cause."
—Lady Gaga

"I've been asked time and again . . . I still don't know exactly what happened. When Miss Taylor came to me wanting to play Velvet I liked her spirit and her looks but she was too small, too short to be convincing as a rider. A few months later she came back, taller—either actually taller or seemingly taller—and was just right for the part."
—*National Velvet* producer Pandro S. Berman

"For years I thought Velvet was the name of the horse . . . I must not have been paying attention. I was mesmerized by Elizabeth Taylor and how she looked, even as a little girl. Years later I found out she was playing someone named Velvet Brown [in *National Velvet*]."
—Isabella Rossellini [*Blue Velvet*]

"She was really a child of nature. All those wonderful movies as a child star with animals and wide-open spaces. And then several Earth Mother roles. . . . Several of her movie titles refer to animals; I don't think that's a coincidence."
—animal-activist Betty White

"Mickey Rooney was billed first in *National Velvet*. He'd been a major star. . . . Perhaps he saw this as a comeback, or perhaps another animal-oriented picture. He didn't take Elizabeth seriously, she was so petite and had a chirrupy voice. What rather threw him was how serious and passionate she was when she acted, while he often focused on entertaining himself and the crew. Elizabeth's role was the standout. Mickey thought his was, by virtue of his starring in it. He was more than surprised at the result."
—Clarence Brown, the film's director

"I've teased Elizabeth that she first made a hit as a girl pretending to be a boy. In *National Velvet* she breaks the rule against female jockeys by impersonating a boy, and she wins the race over the real ones. Of course she's disqualified, but she's made her point. It was a movie ahead of its time."
—costar Jackie "Butch" Jenkins

"I was the star of *Lassie, Come Home*, Elizabeth's second picture. Almost everyone in it was British, it was like a family. I've been asked whether I felt competitive with Elizabeth or thought she might steal our scenes together. No. None of that. We were instantly friends. She was charming and sincere. Sincerity has never been a Hollywood hallmark."
—Roddy McDowall

"MGM was surprised by Elizabeth's success in *National Velvet*. But then they kept her off the screen for some time, unsure what to do with her. Finally they starred her in *Courage of Lassie*. She hadn't yet blossomed, you see. The next picture, she got her initiation into kissing, and since then her kissing scenes have been legion. Millions of girls learned how to kiss well from watching Elizabeth Taylor do it."

—costume designer and friend Edith Head

"When Vivien Leigh played Cleopatra in the film of Shaw's *Caesar and Cleopatra*, she came across as a bubbleheaded nymphet. Leigh displayed none of the moxie she did as Scarlett O'Hara. . . . Elizabeth Taylor's was a modern, politically astute Cleopatra who used two powerful Roman leaders to try and rule or co-rule the Mediterranean world."

—historian Barbara Tuchman

"That scene in which Cleopatra makes her triumphal entry into Rome is beyond . . . well, just spectacular. I doubt there's one scene in any other movie that matches it for sheer impressive splendor. It's more than spectacular."
—Tina Louise (*Gilligan's Island*)

"*Caesar and Cleopatra* became the most expensive British film, then *Cleopatra* became the most expensive Hollywood film. The latter was so costly that it was almost a year after completion until its release. Meanwhile, a small army of contending executives tried to shape all that pricy celluloid into a not-too-long, not-too-short, commercial-enough version. If nobody had shown up to see *Cleopatra*, if its total cost had gone unrecouped, that could have spelled the end of the Fox studio." —film distributor Harry Walders

"I have nothing against Italians but they supported Mussolini and lost the war [WWII]. So in the 1960s poverty was still widespread. *Cleopatra* brought lots of employment to the Rome area. . . . One of the myriad ways the film's budget went up was locals ripping costumes to shreds so they had to be remade, which could take weeks. . . . The extras often didn't appear when required—they did show up on pay days. . . . More sabotage . . . you name it. It wasn't all about Elizabeth Taylor's poor health."

—producer Walter Wanger

"The press had gone in for such excessive and constant coverage during the making of *Cleopatra* that when it actually reached the cinemas, critics and anyone who wished to seem sophisticated had to pan it. You'd be Pollyanna if you didn't say oh-no or at least ho-hum. . . . The public didn't care what the critics said, they wanted to see Liz and Dick and what all the hubbub was about with this movie." —*San Mateo Times* writer Barbara Bladen

"Some moral watchdog groups warned their followers that *Cleopatra* contained 'casual' nudity. In one all-female scene Elizabeth Taylor is lying facedown on a massage table, her back covered but her side, from face to feet, nude. If you want to call that nude. At the time, many people wanted to. That's the most 'nudity' Elizabeth Taylor ever showed on screen. She didn't need to peel to be sexy or seductive. It came from her eyes and her attitude, not to mention being so naturally voluptuous."—*Cleopatra* costar Hume Cronyn

"I remember when she played the prostitute in *Butterfield 8* there was a lot of fuss. In previous movies, when a character was a prostitute, it was camouflaged. . . . Several movie critics were indignant that her character would only have sex with men she herself chose. Apparently they'd have preferred a character who had no choice."

—Natalie Wood

"It didn't occur to me then that *A Place in the Sun* was about anything but class differences. Monty Clift's character aspired to the upper class through Elizabeth's character. *After* he got involved with my working-class character. Today some people say the movie espoused reproductive freedom, since my character's not being able to get a legal abortion leads to her death and then to Monty's. You should know that the original novel by Theodore Dreiser had a different, more descriptive title: *An American Tragedy*."

—Shelley Winters

"After the film of my novel became such a hit, it was suggested I do a distaff version. A differing plot, different situations, but with a Godmother. Who, I asked, would play this singular role? The backers said Elizabeth Taylor. I declined. Miss Taylor might have *looked* the part . . . [but] she was not capable of playing Italian and her voice was wrong for the part. Ideal casting would have been Anna Magnani, who was too old by Hollywood standards and not box office in the U.S. Later on, Taylor somewhat resembled Magnani."
—*The Godfather* author Mario Puzo

"It's been printed numerous times that I resemble Elizabeth Taylor. I know it's meant as a compliment . . . I do not have the same abiding interest in men that she does. Our voices are also quite distinct. I scare off a lot of men whose voices aren't deeper than mine."
—actress Suzanne Pleshette

"One misses the opportunity of working with Miss Taylor. . . . We do share the same mole, and very few men have one there. Mine is real, as is hers. If mine weren't real, I wouldn't have had one put on."

—Robert Vaughn (*Hustle*)

"Everyone always says what beautiful eyes I have, then half the time they'll say I have 'Elizabeth Taylor eyes.' Or comment that I look like her, with the eyes and black hair . . . and when it comes to gaining a bit of extra weight, even more comparisons. I'll tell you something: no actress very much relishes comparisons with another actress."

—Delta Burke (*Designing Women*)

"If you want to devote the best part of four hours to looking at Elizabeth Taylor in all her draped and undraped physical splendor, then this is your movie. In royal regalia, *en negligee*, or *au naturel*, she gives the impression that she is at one of Miami Beach's more exotic resorts."

—from the *New York Herald Tribune*'s review of *Cleopatra*

"It's reached the point where any actress applying a beauty spot to the lower half of her face is accused of copying Elizabeth Taylor! For all I know, Miss Taylor has been copying someone else, and I certainly had a famous mole some time before Miss Taylor did."

—British star Margaret Lockwood (*The Wicked Lady*)

"To act opposite Elizabeth Taylor is rather mesmerizing when you're playing face to face, looking into those eyes. They are beautiful but intimidating eyes . . . no other actor or actress ever kept me on my toes as much as when I had to act opposite those blazing eyes."

—costar Peter Ustinov (*The Comedians*)

"I'd like to know where to place the blame. Whether it's she or he who says, Let's do *this* movie, luv. Burton-Taylor are currently foisting themselves on an incredulous and dwindling public in *Boom!*, a big bust by way of a trivial Tennessee Williams play. That, we can guess is *her* fault—love that Tennessee! A year or so past, the brazen couple did the non-comedy *The Comedians*, via one of Graham Greene's most convoluted and irrelevant tales. One of the two must have said, Ooh, Graham Greene, luv! Mustn't miss a chance to do a Graham Greene, he's veddy, veddy esteemed. Taylor's German accent in *The Comedians* had to be heard to be disbelieved."　　　—British critic Gil Monsen

"I was surprised to hear what impelled Elizabeth Taylor to take the wife/mistress role in *The Comedians* was a rumor that Sophia Loren was going to do it. She didn't want Sophia near Richard, so she snatched the role. . . . How did Miss Taylor think Sophia Loren could possibly enact a German?"　　　—German supermodel Veruschka

"After seeing them so often and so ostentatiously together in real life and in reel life, it's clear that Elizabeth Taylor and Richard Burton have become legends in their own time and in their own minds."
—singer-actor Robert Goulet, who supported
Richard Burton on stage in *Camelot*

"It's still on TV, in reruns, that episode of *Here's Lucy* where she meets Elizabeth Taylor and Richard Burton and she tries on that famous ring [with the Burton-Cartier diamond] and it gets stuck on Lucy's finger. That's an awesome episode."
—Keanu Reeves ("Lucy Meets the Burtons" was the series' highest-rated episode)

"For most of [the *Here's Lucy* episode] Burton impersonated a plumber. . . . In movies he *can* be charming . . . with us he seemed resentful. He certainly resented Lucille. . . . Liz didn't appear till after the middle—the eagerly awaited 'star turn,' as Burton put it. But she wasn't soured like him . . . not even embarrassed to let everyone know that as soon as our taping was over she was heading for the hospital for another operation for 'piles'— hemorrhoids, in American. Good grief."

—Jerry Paris, TV director and former actor (neighbor Jerry on *The Dick Van Dyke Show*)

"I was in Los Angeles with them during the 1970 *Lucy* opening-season episode. Rich was glad, originally, to get on a successful teleseries for a single episode. Nor was he drinking that week. But he and Elizabeth felt rather exploited, as if they were being showcased on Miss Ball's show as an event, to win her ratings. Which was true . . . I think they looked down on television and, furthermore, preferred to control exploitative situations. By another token, they did agree to be on the *Here's Lucy* show."

—Richard Burton's friend and assistant Brook Williams
(son of Welsh actor-playwright Emlyn)

"Richard Burton could be quite the male chauvinist. He came from a redneck background—twelve kids. . . . Lucy is the queen of comedy, she knows the business inside-out and always goes through scenes with her actors and offers suggestions. Precisely how many comedies has Richard Burton ever done? But he only wanted directions from the director, who was Lucy's employee. Directors may call the shots in movies but not in television. Elizabeth was nowhere as tense, she could smile and laugh. . . . He sometimes had murder in his eyes. Odious man."

—Cleo Smith, Lucille Ball's cousin and a *Here's Lucy* producer

"I never understood why Burton did it. Being married to any actress can be distressing. Don't I know. But marriage to a lady or woman richer and more famous than yourself . . . that, I could never subject myself to."

—Sean Connery, whose first wife was actress Diane Cilento

"Elizabeth was more jealous of Richard's leading ladies than he was of her leading men. Not so much because she was afraid he'd pounce on them as that some aggressive, ambitious actress would pounce on him and try and take her place in the Dick-and-Liz media saga."
—Rod Steiger, who eventually dated ET

"Elizabeth Taylor did not want to be displaced. She was aware, and so was Burton, that she'd elevated him from a foreign star to an international superstar. But now he was in a position, if he ever left Taylor, to boost a little-known actress to a star or a star actress to a superstar."

—writer Marvin Jones

"One factor in Elizabeth's doing an uncredited cameo in Richard's *Anne of the Thousand Days* [about Henry VIII and Anne Boleyn] was she liked to play dress-up. The Tudor outfit and headdress looked smashing on her. Another factor was to be on-set, keeping an eye on Richard. More specifically, on Genevieve Bujold, the young leading lady. The French-Canadian actress hadn't made it big in Hollywood yet."

—Sian Phillips, actress and wife of Peter O'Toole

"When Elizabeth was making *The Only Game in Town* opposite Warren Beatty, Richard would harp on Warren's good looks. She insisted they were like sister and kid brother. Richard kept insisting Warren was a temptation . . . I doubt she and Warren did anything but chat. Both of them love to hold forth . . . maybe it was all competing monologues."
—writer Sheridan Morley

"We had no idea [*What Ever Happened to*] *Baby Jane* would become a big success, though the story was dynamite . . . I felt Bette [Davis] should have won a third Oscar . . . what she did with the role was unique. Had there been a big-screen remake, I feel the sole actress capable of stepping into Davis's strap shoes would be Elizabeth Taylor. She's now the right age for it."   —Henry Farrell, author of the novel on which the film was based

"I had a project Liz Taylor would have suited, and vice versa. But she'd been so exploited by her studio that once she was free to make fewer movies, she did. And after the very time-consuming *Cleopatra* she signed for fewer projects, particularly without her hubby, who was busy shuttling from picture to picture."
—*Baby Jane* director-producer Robert Aldrich

"She was known to turn down good scripts because she didn't want to leave Richard's side and to choose, when she did choose, second-rate projects, like the one [*The Driver's Seat*, aka *Identikit*] from Muriel Spark, who'd written *The Prime of Miss Jean Brodie*. Elizabeth placed too much importance on past authorship and prestigious reputation, and not enough on the script in hand."   —magazine editor Ingrid Sischy

"*Taming of the Shrew* had been a big hit, so decades later she agreed to work again with [director] Franco Zeffirelli in *Young Toscanini* . . . to try and re-capture some of the old box-office magic. But the biopic was a boring flop, all superfice and no substance. One critic said it was likelier to please those familiar with a chocolate box than an opera box. It bombed in Europe and would have in the USA except it hardly played even New York or L.A."
                                        —Richard Gully, former assistant to Jack L. Warner

"Her fulfilling marriages were to Mike Todd and Richard Burton. During those times she was usually content to let movies go hang. Elizabeth kept busy traveling with and usually sticking like glue to those two men. She always had to have something going on. If it wasn't a movie or a man, it was . . . campaigning for one husband or raising funds to fight AIDS, the perfume business . . . but always something. Because when Elizabeth is bored or down she eats too much."
                                        —fellow MGM contractee June Allyson

"At about seven, Elizabeth's parents moved her and her older brother to Los Angeles, and by age ten Sara Taylor had gotten her into pictures. Mama's job was carting Elizabeth to one audition after another. . . . Before long, Elizabeth's income was supporting the family. That only inspired Sara to aim even higher."
                                        —friend, costar, and MGM colleague Peter Lawford

"One of Elizabeth's heroines, growing up, was Bette Davis during her golden age as the 'fifth Warner Brother.' Bette was attractive then, but not so much so that her looks boxed her into decorative roles. . . . Bette got the best scripts and alternated between likeable and popular characters and unlikable ones in popular films. Elizabeth, like most actresses, admired and aspired to that."
                                        —costar Louis Jourdan (*The V.I.P.s*)

"Elizabeth took after her mother. . . . Sara was the mover and shaker in the family, the restless and dissatisfied one—the pushy one. Elizabeth's father Francis loved art. He was quiet and polite. Nobody had an unkind word to say about him. Which couldn't quite be said about mother and daughter."   —MGM composer Hugh Martin

"It's no secret now that Francis Taylor was the longtime boyfriend of [MGM costume designer] Adrian. Both men had wives for cover—Adrian's was Janet Gaynor, who was bi or lesbian and the first actress to win an Academy Award. And both men reproduced—Adrian and Janet had a son, the Taylors had two children. But that didn't change their nature . . . both preferred sex with men."

—actor and Goldwyn contractee Farley Granger

"We've lived the same life: the great tragedy of childhood stars. . . .
My father took the money."
—Michael Jackson (ET's father did not take her money)

"Was Elizabeth hypnotized or what? Going on Barbara Walters, defending Michael Jackson's relationships with boys under fourteen, and then, because Walters mentions that Jackson's father used to beat him and wonders if Elizabeth's also beat her, Elizabeth nods yes! Her brother denies it, so does anyone who knew the family. Why does Elizabeth choose to identify so completely with that guy? And why on earth besmirch and betray the memory of her father?"   —publicist Ronni Chasen

"Elizabeth's more recent operations, since about age sixty, including 'upstairs,' have . . . taken something away—they've had a marked effect. Sometimes she slurs her words or doesn't make sense . . . she's not the same, physically or mentally, as she was before."

—ET friend and photographer Herb Ritts

"It's not so much growing older as the cumulative effect of operation after operation, as well as the volume of medications. In her early sixties Elizabeth started experiencing awful headaches . . . and suddenly, memory loss. A brand-new affliction. She would ask friends, 'What fresh hell is this?'"

—writer-producer Marvin Jones

"A star actress ultimately works less if she only accepts leads. Else, she retires from acting to find a new field of endeavor. Or retires, period. Or—what the true actor does—takes smaller roles and does the best of what's on offer, including television so long as it's not too infra dig. Elizabeth has been working less, not by choice. The only thing that curbs her energy is ill health, which often does interrupt."

—UK director Guy Hamilton (*The Mirror Crack'd*)

"Eleven years between her two final marriages, and during that time Elizabeth was eager to work. . . . Many fans were disappointed to see her in minor roles, for instance a brothel madam in a TV offering titled *North and South*. . . . Elizabeth can keep herself in the headlines but not up on the screen. That's out of her hands."

—columnist Radie Harris (ET earned $100,000 for one day's work in the miniseries)

"Depending on the source, Elizabeth Taylor earned half a million bucks or one million for her three weeks in *Malice in Wonderland*, a TV movie about [gossip columnists] Hedda Hopper and Louella Parsons. . . . Liz had a field day playing her old enemy Louella and using Louella's whiny baby voice."   —*Malice* costar Joyce Van Patten (Dick's sister)

"What's caught up with Elizabeth Taylor is her tardiness. A yen for attention is one thing, gifts and bribes another . . . but consistently holding up production, whether from bad health or feelings or a mood, is inexcusable. This is first and foremost a business."

—George C. Scott

"By the time I worked with her [in 1950] Miss Taylor had matured or erupted from a determined but proper English-type girl into young leads as a raven-haired, lavender-eyed beauty whose screen presence was phenomenal. . . . The amount of attention she was getting on and off screen turned her head. How could it fail to do so?"

—ET's director Vincente Minnelli (*Father of the Bride* and *Father's Little Dividend*)

"You know, her eyes are not really violet. That is publicity. As Elizabeth herself says, her eyes change color according to what she wears."
—costar Fernando Lamas (*The Girl Who Had Everything*)

"She's changed markedly from when she played my naïve young bride in our picture [*Conspirator*, 1949]. I would not have thought her capable of the behavior she's displayed since her third or fourth marriage. I do not condone her behavior."

—Robert Taylor in 1963

"Before final casting of *Conspirator*, a McCarthy-era witch hunt type of MGM picture, there was real concern in the head office. Robert Taylor and Elizabeth Taylor—same last name, both black-haired . . . might the public think *incest*? . . . I heard some polls were taken to reassure Louis B. Mayer that it was okay to cast both Taylors in the same picture."
—director Stanley Donen

"Soon after [WWII] Elizabeth was one of the players ordered to travel to Washington, D.C., to help launch the March of Dimes campaign. She got to meet the president but told her mom she didn't like Truman because he looked like Louis B. Mayer. He didn't, though, not by about thirty pounds."   —Don Taylor, ET's groom in *Father of the Bride*

"I didn't see *Father of the Bride* or its sequel until Elizabeth half-jokingly encouraged me. Too bad that both centered not on her but the hokey, cheapskate father enacted—indifferently, maybe because of his alcoholism—by Spencer Tracy. . . . Those pictures were sizeable hits, so Elizabeth's big fear at the time was that they might become a series. Being associated with a film series was death for an ambitious star."
—Halston, designer and ET pal

"I could have wished Elizabeth Taylor had protested the post-war backlash against democracy in our country. But older and bigger names didn't, or felt they didn't dare. In or out of Hollywood, people were terrorized. McCarthyites used intimidation tactics, including guilt by association. And we had a president [Truman] who kept silent about what was going on."
—blacklisted Anne Revere, a descendant of Paul Revere, who played ET's mother in *National Velvet* and Monty Clift's mother in *A Place in the Sun*

"Elizabeth is or was, for the longest time, politically ingenuous. She evinced no interest in politics and would rub shoulders with political reactionaries—including the enemies of her gay friends—if it was a gala occasion or the funeral of a rich friend. Her worldview isn't very broad . . . poverty, over-population, and government manipulation aren't much in her purview."   —actor and Screen Actors Guild president William Schallert

"She admits to a minimal education. The little schoolhouse at MGM
was little more than a joke, a minimal compliance with the law.
Elizabeth is, however, very worldly wise about feelings and
people and making her way in the world.
We can all learn a thing or two from her."
—Richard Burton

"I met her a few times in her teens . . . she did seem aloof and more or less impatient to be elsewhere. Years later when we were in *Raintree County* she was more pleasant and paid attention when you conversed. I assume that marriage, motherhood, and intermittent unhappiness had given her depth and compassion."
—Tom Drake, best known for *Meet Me in St. Louis*

"Like most of us educated at Metro, Elizabeth wishes she had a more literate background. . . . Even after you become famous there's still a part of you that feels left out or a little embarrassed when you're in the company of people who went to college. Fame and fortune makes up for a lot . . . not everything."
—Ann Miller, dancer-actress and MGM contractee

"Elizabeth Taylor does read books now and again. Richard Burton is very book-oriented and would rather be a famous author than a famous actor. He's introduced her to better books, to non-fiction. But they often read mystery novels together. She does prefer fiction. Especially things with strong female roles."

—ET's director Joseph Losey (*Secret Ceremony*)

"Elizabeth has a good instinct for material. When she was reading *The Godfather* I asked what was it like, it was such a big bestseller. She said it was poorly written but almost impossible to put down. . . . One script she was reading, I asked what it was about. Elizabeth threw it down in disgust. 'It's about all I can take!' That script was later filmed, with a top actress, and flopped badly."

—Brook Williams, sometime actor and companion to Richard Burton

"As an actress, a businesswoman, and as a woman, one of Elizabeth Taylor's best bargaining tricks is playing hard to get. She does it very well. It's not really a trick because she never cares that much if you get her or not. If you do, it will be on her own terms."

—singer Julio Iglesias

"We wooed Elizabeth with favorable conditions and gifts. And more gifts. Virtually every day of shooting, she was gifted—more accurately, she was a gifted actress who didn't need to work and could buy most anything her heart desired, but Elizabeth was accustomed to and even expected that we give her a gift—some expensive bauble, an antique, or a piece of jewelry—to thank her for completing a day's filming and to show our appreciation. Elizabeth very much likes to be appreciated."   —Renée Valente, producer of ET's western telefilm *Poker Alice*

"My goodness! I don't begrudge her, I only wish I was treated the same way as Elizabeth Taylor any time I make a television movie. You'd have thought she was starring in a big-budget motion picture . . . I guess they think she deserves it, and who am I to say she doesn't?"
—Patty Duke

"What's happening is that most big-name male actors won't go near Liz Taylor on big or little screen. They don't care to be overshadowed. She relegates most of her leading men to near-supporting status. So even in TV projects she doesn't get the top TV actors, she gets middle-level actors or has-been movie actors. They know who'll get the juicy role with the big build-up and all the publicity."
—columnist Lee Graham

"I have directed [Brigitte] Bardot, [Catherine] Deneuve, [Jane] Fonda . . . I would like to make a romantic fantasy with Elizabeth Taylor, preferably in Europe. But I know even there she will finish by directing me, and that must not be."
—French director Roger Vadim

"*Suddenly, Last Summer* showed that Taylor could act. But three other movies saw to it that she would never play anything but a sexpot—*Cat on a Hot Tin Roof*, *Butterfield 8*, and *Cleopatra*. She'd have had a more varied career if she'd not chosen roles that made so much of her figure and characters that live and breathe for love. She didn't do any of that in *Suddenly, Last Summer*."
—Gore Vidal

"Taylor's career was in danger of being eclipsed by her private life and public scandals until the humongous budget of *Cleopatra* and its sheer optical splendor reminded everyone that this was a truly major movie star. . . . Her alliance with Burton and their movies together gave her career a new lease on life. Until it dragged them both down, pretty much for keeps."
                                                    —film historian Carlos Clarens

"Everyone hated *A Little Night Music* [the film version]. I liked it better than the Broadway musical that everyone loved. I think it was great they hired Liz Taylor, who can't sing. It's a big movie tradition, like when they hired Lucy Ball for *Mame*. . . . Liz is brave. She sang 'Send in the Clowns' by herself, no dubbing. You could right away tell it was really her."   —Andy Warhol, who appeared in ET's *The Driver's Seat*, aka *Identikit*

"Due to her box-office stature Elizabeth Taylor was seriously considered for the movie of *Hello, Dolly!* Never mind her non-singing status. Yes, Barbra Streisand was too young for the part, but thank goodness they chose her instead. My musical score has never been sung more beautifully."
                                        —composer-lyricist Jerry Herman

"Liz Taylor practically died laughing when she heard she was up for the motion picture of my *Myra Breckinridge*. 'Me play an ex-man?' she gasped. She couldn't decide whether it was hilarious or insulting. Liz was a little too ripe for the role. Raquel Welch was just right in age, looks, and synthetic appeal. Rex Reed, the bitchy movie critic, played the man, as it were, that she used to be."
                                                    —novelist Gore Vidal

"She had to sing 'Send in the Clowns,' which terrified her. 'Every great singer has done it,' she said, 'and now here comes Chunko.' She gained fifteen pounds during this production."
—ET biographer J. Randy Taraborrelli

"Elizabeth Taylor is five years older than Warren Beatty. However, in *The Only Game in Town* she appears a decade or more his senior. Her image and physical self have grown increasingly blowsy. As a Las Vegas chorine she is baldly unbelievable. She must have assumed this picture would amount to something due to the guiding presence of her *Giant* director George Stevens. But he too must be past it. By any objective standard, the result is a neon-colored catastrophe."   —British columnist Gillian Dawes

"I was sorry *The Only Game in Town* didn't work out. The ingredients sounded promising . . . just that the most crucial one wasn't included—a good, solid story. *Giant* could have been made with unknown actors and it would still be a good story."
—Rock Hudson

"Appearing in *Cleopatra* was an unmatchable experience. Just seeing what Elizabeth would look like each day—the costumes and makeup were more than extravagant. . . . Elizabeth had little to do with the script but I wish my character had been less wimpy, regardless of his historical sexuality [bisexual]. For that matter, Caesar was bisexual, but either he was scripted differently or Rex [Harrison] had him, shall we say, beefed up."
—Roddy McDowall

"Has ever a film star been more indulged than Elizabeth Taylor? Of late she insisted that *Reflections in a Golden Eye*, a story set in the American South, be shot in Rome at tremendous extra cost. Then she signed for *The Only Game in Town*, set in Las Vegas but filmed in Paris at her royal command, with specially-built sets representing American casinos, streets, apartments, and a supermarket, adding tremendously to the picture's budget. Almost needless to say, both were flops. Do Hollywood studios never learn from past experiences with Liz? Did *Cleopatra* count for nothing? Are they besotted or mesmerized by Liz Taylor and the chance to star her in yet another overblown money-loser? Or is it really about tax write-offs? What gives?"   —director Lewis Allen

"What other movie queen would have, or does now, take such un-Hollywood-like chances with her glamour? She probably knows less about Stanislavski than Natalie Wood, yet she became old and fat for *Virginia Woolf* and now tops it off with being simpleminded as Leonora."
—writer Gloria Steinem in a note to producer Ray Stark about his
Reflections in a Golden Eye

"She's said the actress she most admires is the Italian movie star Anna Magnani, known for her earthiness and spontaneity. She also admires Miss Magnani's gravelly voice."
—Dick Hanley, ET's secretary

"She is generous to her friends. Roddy McDowall was a child star who isn't an adult star . . . he grew from sweet to acerbic. But Elizabeth secured him the plum role of Octavian, the future Roman emperor Augustus, in *Cleopatra*. I, for one, wasn't as fortunate."
—*Cleopatra* costar Robert Stephens

"I was paid $125,000, although no one ever told me what my job was.
My job description was primarily 'Elizabeth's husband.'
I was to be there just in case she needed me, and to make sure
that she got to the set on time and prepared. All Elizabeth had
to do to earn her salary was act in the picture [*Cleopatra*].
I had to take care of Elizabeth.
As it turned out, she had the easier job."
—Eddie Fisher

"*Cleopatra* was to have been two films. It was enough of a life for three. The real Cleopatra had more than the one sibling . . . her brothers and sisters conspired to kill each other to attain the throne, and Cleopatra herself engaged in fratricide. . . . The film includes only her child by Julius Caesar . . . she and Mark Anthony had three children, including twins. . . . By the way, Anthony, unlike Caesar, was entirely heterosexual and fell too much under Cleopatra's spell for his own good." —Richard Burton

"If you can imagine, 20th Century-Fox executives were afraid the Taylor-Burton affair would harm *Cleopatra*'s box office once it was finally completed. *Au contraire*, the public fascination with the pair's developing relationship in Rome was their best possible advertising." —Italian producer Franco Rossellini

"After *Virginia Woolf*, Elizabeth Taylor would have done well to act apart from Burton and pursue serious British films rather than bloated, hollow Hollywood projects whose lack of artistic and financial success only served to down-grade her." —UK director John Boulting

"There were hopes of Richard Burton returning to the stage, here in England. . . . We were all well pleased when he filmed a student production of *Doctor Faustus*, acted in it gratis, and donated the profits to the Oxford Playhouse. The participation of his wife as Helen of Troy was a splendid bonus and a generous one, inasmuch as she had no speaking lines."

—Frank Hauser, theater director

"They couldn't win for losing. They did *Faustus* as a goodwill gesture. However, the British press generally felt Richard, who co-directed, was being condescending and that Elizabeth's glamorous cameo appearances were sheer vanity. The reviews were scathing."
—Sir John Gielgud

"Richard Burton wanted to do a popular Shakespeare movie—a tall order. He and Elizabeth Taylor invested heavily in *The Taming of the Shrew*. . . . Problems arose when she insisted on Hollywood designer Irene Sharaff to do her costumes. A compromise was reached when Burton didn't care who did his . . . he preferred authenticity."

—Richard Burton biographer Alexander Walker

"The Burtons gave Zeffirelli his first chance to direct a movie, and an A-list one. At first he was so happy, nodding, smiling, grateful, but then . . . it reminds me of Mark Twain's remark that the difference between a man and a dog is if you take a dog in and feed it and clothe it and make it rich, it won't turn on you. Zeffirelli's personality and habits kept him from becoming a Hollywood director, yet who does he blame for that? He's said it various times: 'those Hollywood Jews.' Yeah, like Elizabeth Taylor, who once accepted a first-time unknown director."

—director Gene Saks

"Before filming of *Shrew* began, Burton took their director to meet Philip Burton, who would authenticate details and answer questions about the production. Richard clearly still idolized the man whose surname he took. . . . It became the first Shakespeare-based hit movie in decades."   —Emlyn Williams, Welsh actor and playwright

"Richard was dying to do *The Taming of the Shrew*. He talked Elizabeth into it . . . and into waiving, as he did, her usual sizeable acting fee. Instead, they took a percentage. Richard told me, 'I don't think the concept of doing a film for the love of it had ever occurred to her before.'"   —UK journalist Michael Munn

"Elizabeth now really loathes him, largely because he is a ruthless selfish multi-faced ego-mad *coward*. It is this last that both of us find most objectionable. I am by no means heroic morally but I can make decisions and accept advice. This chap can do neither."
—from Richard Burton's diary entry for April 27, 1966, referencing
Taming of the Shrew director Franco Zeffirelli

"There was always, at that time, grousing about how much Elizabeth Taylor and Richard Burton were earning. Naturally she earned more for *Who's Afraid of Virginia Woolf?* than *Cleopatra*, which had been years earlier. . . . Our picture ran over schedule by some thirty days, which contractually meant they were to be paid an extra million dollars between them. They simply waived the overtime."   —*Woolf* screenwriter Ernest Lehman

"Working with them was extraordinary. They were like royalty and yet Richard was so approachable. They called each other names. I think it was in fun."
—*Woolf* costar Sandy Dennis

"The whole cast was Oscar-nominated—the two women, the two men. The two women won."

—screenwriter and AMPAS (Academy of Motion Picture Arts and Sciences) president Fay Kanin

"Only the two of them could know how closely, or not, George and Martha paralleled their own lives. But it does seem as if the longer they were together the more they put each other down, in jest or otherwise."

—Irish actor Richard Harris, one of whose wives later wed Rex Harrison

"You knew the Liz-and-Dick globe-trotting caravan and circus had gotten out of hand when they let themselves be cast for big-big bucks in a movie of a flop Tennessee Williams play retitled *Boom!* The play had starred old Tallulah Bankhead and sexpot Tab Hunter. She's rich and dying, he's a young poet and the angel of death. The film casting made no sense, with Taylor too young and Burton too old. *Boom!* was a total fiasco and the beginning of their end, their last major costarring effort and the stop to each of them as a top box-office attraction."

—novelist and biographer Gavin Lambert

"Elizabeth holds a fierce dedication to the work of Tennessee Williams, owing to her successes in *Cat on a Hot Tin Roof* and *Suddenly, Last Summer*. . . . She failed to discern the skimpiness of his play *The Milk Train Doesn't Stop Here Any More*, which made a skimpily plotted if lavish motion picture. I was paid handsomely but blushed deeply and often upon the film's fierce rejection."

—Sir Noël Coward, who played the Witch of Capri in *Boom!*

"They said some really nasty things to each other." —*Woolf* director Mike Nichols

"Those who've suggested Miss Taylor would do better to work apart from her husband will have to reconsider. The year [1968] has seen her opposite the equally miscast Richard Burton in *Boom!* and minus Burton in the incomprehensible *Secret Ceremony*. Both mystifying. Both misfires, and then some." —writer Helene Hanff

"In *Secret Ceremony* Liz Taylor shares a large bathtub with Mia Farrow. What does this mean? The film never clarifies the relationship . . . mother-daughter? sapphic? a hallucination? . . . Robert Mitchum is extraneous, tossed in—not into the tub—for the traditional sake of including a leading man. A nasty one." —writer Arthur Bell

"I believe Elizabeth's salary was back down to $1 million. However, Mitchum only received $150,000 and Mia Farrow, really the central character, got $75,000." —*Secret Ceremony* director Joseph Losey

"We paid Elizabeth Taylor $1.4 million but *The Only Game in Town* [1969] lost almost $6 million." —producer Fred Kohlmar

"The '70s is thus far Miss Taylor's worst decade as an actress. Where once Richard Burton shared a platonic but kingly bed with Peter O'Toole in the historic *Becket*, she now, in a small role, shares a boozy bed with O'Toole in *Under Milk Wood* [1971]. . . . In *Hammersmith Is Out* [1972] she dons a blonde wig as a Southern slattern named Jimmie Jean Jackson. How long into her forties shall Elizabeth Taylor reappear in whore-ible movies?" —film critic Aimee Martin

"The distintegration of Elizabeth Taylor has been a very sad thing to stand by helplessly and watch. Something ghastly has happened over the course of her last four or five films. She has become a hideous parody of herself—a fat, sloppy, yelling, screeching banshee."

—film critic Rex Reed

"It isn't really about weight gain. The medications Elizabeth is given for her sciatica and other ailments bloat her face, they make her puffy. Strangers assume she's eating too much. . . . One doctor ordered her to stay flat on her back for a month. She can't do that. Within days she was out and about, dining with Dick and the Duke and Duchess of Windsor in London."

—ET's secretary Roger Wall

"Rich worries about the amount of alcohol Elizabeth consumes along with the drugs she's given to ease the pain . . . or after an operation. Elizabeth mixes booze and drugs in as large or larger quantities than did Marilyn Monroe. Rich believes he will eventually die from drink while Elizabeth will sail blithely on. He dislikes the sometimes necessary role of being her caregiver."

—Richard Burton's assistant Brook Williams

"After another big blow-out Richard went on a bender in Switzerland, partly to get back at Elizabeth. He took his favorite brother, Ifor, who'd been a coal miner. . . . Richard's mother died before he was two, and his father was a coal miner who condemned acting as a profession. The bender ended suddenly when Ifor, the equally sloshed elder brother, slipped and broke his neck. Ifor was paralyzed from the neck down for the rest of his life. Richard blamed himself, justly."

—Sir Michael Redgrave

"He had so much, yet he was alcoholic before, during, and after Elizabeth Taylor. The periods of sobriety were few and his attempts to give up drinking were halfhearted or at any rate temporary. After the death of his brother Ifor in 1972 he made no further efforts to stop."

—MGM hairdresser and ET confidant Sydney Guilaroff

"Thank goodness she accompanied Richard to our Austrian location. She was like an assistant to me . . . invaluable. She sometimes kept Richard from drinking, and when he did drink was able to order him to do things he didn't want to do. One day, he was so inebriated he thought a required wooden prop was actually high explosives. Richard kept insisting he wouldn't touch it. We sent for Elizabeth . . . she arrived and yelled at him to get it over with and do the f---ing scene. And he did it. They were a great couple."

—Brian Hutton, director of *Where Eagles Dare*, for which Richard Burton was paid $1 million (several times more than costar Clint Eastwood)

"Richard would drink solo or in company but Elizabeth didn't like to drink alone. The problem was, when he was trying not to drink he sometimes fell off the wagon because she brought along a pitcher of martinis for lunch and would insist that he join her."

—Peter Ustinov, their director and costar in *Hammersmith Is Out*

"Elizabeth and I both suffer from feelings of insecurity. We feel particularly unsure of ourselves when we are at a party because no one really wants to know us. They simply stare as if we are prize animals. What we do when we go to parties is drink to kill the icy isolation."

—Richard Burton

"Elizabeth is wonderful company if you're not around her for very long. Only because of the drinking and the attention span."
—British actor Stewart Granger

"That whole generation of men didn't want working or successful wives. Marilyn Monroe's marriage to Joe DiMaggio lasted under a year because he wanted her to give up her career, move to San Francisco, become a housewife, and cook Italian meals for his relatives. Richard grew more and more jealous of Elizabeth's career. He was making more films than her but nagged that she should work even less, that she'd already made her mark. . . . She had two Oscars and he was not pleased to become the actor most often nominated for Academy Awards without ever winning one. Even John Wayne, that eminent thespian, won an Oscar—in competition with Richard Burton!"
—Lynn Redgrave

"Elizabeth had a long, productive career. She was the most glamorous star of our generation. No one else could equal Elizabeth's beauty and sexuality. Women liked her and men adored her, including my husband [Eddie Fisher]. Her love for her children is enduring. She was a symbol of stardom. Her legacy will last."
—Debbie Reynolds's press statement upon ET's death

CHAPTER 3

The Siren

"Every minute this broad spends out of bed is a waste of time."

—ET's third husband, Mike Todd

"I once asked Elizabeth Taylor how she felt about being tagged 'the most beautiful woman in the world.' She answered, 'Oh, that's just silly. I see better-looking women every day just walking down the street.'"

—photographer Tom Gates

"It's true. She has no idea how beautiful she is. . . . Shortly after she was born the doctor gave us a good scare. The doctor told us she had a mutation. Well, that sounded just awful—a mutation. But he explained that her eyes had double rows of eyelashes."

—Sara Taylor

"Elizabeth was not a born beauty. At birth she was enveloped in a down of soft brown hair . . . residual hypertrichosis. Fortunately the down covering her whole body faded or fell away with time, and her dramatic black and white coloring emerged."

—MGM hairdresser Sydney Guilaroff

"Most beautiful? Maybe. Sexiest? Very possibly."
—actor George C. Scott

"(She) was the funniest-looking baby I had ever seen! Her hair was long and black. Her ears were covered with thick black fuzz and inlaid into the sides of her head . . . and her tiny face was so tightly closed it looked as if it would never unfold."
—from a 1954 *McCall's* magazine article by Sara Taylor

"You look at a photo of the Taylor children, and Howard, a blond, was more beautiful than Elizabeth. His mum said he looked like a Botticelli angel. But Sara didn't push him into show business. She saved all her efforts for Elizabeth."   —friend Peter Lawford

"She preferred Elizabeth to me or my dad. She was our mother's favorite. I didn't mind. Our mother had her involved in singing and dancing lessons by age two. . . . When she was little I nicknamed her Lizzie the Lizard, and she's disliked being called Liz ever since. Both our grandmothers were named Elizabeth."   —Howard Taylor

"Elizabeth's middle name, Rosemond, was her father's mother's maiden or birth name . . . a beautiful name, don't you think? When I played her older sister in *National Velvet* I would sometimes stare at Elizabeth. She was already beautiful, yet different in appearance from anyone else. Ages later we were together in an all-star Agatha Christie adaptation [*The Mirror Crack'd*]. I played the amateur sleuth Miss Marple, so hair and makeup aged me beyond what I looked. Elizabeth had become somewhat hefty but she was still very striking. . . . It was like rekindling an old friendship."   —Angela Lansbury

"When Elizabeth Taylor became fat it was like a desecration. Most great beauties cling to their looks to a great or an even greater degree. But long before old age, to throw them away, to literally devour them out of existence . . . it was sad and shocking."
—Oscar-winning French actress Simone Signoret

"When you've been a child star and then you become a young woman there is a delayed reaction. You're used to being seen and treated as a child. At most a precocious adolescent. So when your figure finally begins causing attention from boys, it might take a while to notice it. Or to be sure it's you . . . and to become secure about your looks. I know."
—Peggy Ann Garner (*A Tree Grows in Brooklyn*)

"Elizabeth was already pretty. She was never a tomboy, even though she loved riding horses. What changed was . . . well, her figure. She came *out* . . . and I gave her her first screen kiss. It was a big publicity deal at the time. "
—Jimmy Lydon, her romantic interest in *Cynthia* (1947)

"Insiders half expected a secret sexual liaison between *Giant* costars Rock Hudson and James Dean. For various reasons, it didn't happen. Hudson disliked Dean's rudeness and competitiveness . . . and his sullen temperament. Dean thought Rock was a handsome no-talent and may have resented how well-endowed Hudson was, since rumor had it that James Dean wasn't exactly a *big* star. Elizabeth was happy to flirt with both men, each vying for her platonic attention against the other man. . . . Had Rock and Jimmy had an affair, you can surmise she'd have felt rather left out."
—ET's secretary Dick Hanley

"James Dean was ambitious but not intent on a cover-up marriage. Like Rock Hudson, he'd probably have stayed contractually single until forced to marry, to squelch the true rumors. . . . Elizabeth Taylor had a crush on him. Years later, she said, 'He and I . . . "twinkled." We had a . . . well, a little "twinkle" for each other.'"

—Richard Barr, stage producer of *Who's Afraid of Virginia Woolf?*

"Elizabeth kept playing daughters in film after film, so there was this look-but-don't-touch status she retained. It wasn't until she played young marrieds or not-quite-yet-marrieds that she was marketed as a budding sex symbol. MGM was a more prudish studio than most."

—casting director turned producer Renée Valente

"Metro sensed what a valuable asset they had in a grown-up Liz Taylor. When she divorced 'Nicky' Hilton it was a scandal merely because divorce itself was a scandal then. The awful truth, the *why*, wasn't known. . . . Metro would have preferred Liz to stay single after the divorce, but when she remarried they were relieved it wasn't some young Romeo, let alone one with a famous surname."

—columnist Mike Connolly

"MGM was glad to put Michael Wilding under contract when Elizabeth Taylor took him as her new husband. He was classy and well-mannered . . . he could be depended upon. They knew he was giving up a starring career in England for his new young wife. . . . He never did reach stardom in Hollywood, and when he left almost nobody noticed."

—columnist James Bacon

"Joan Crawford's old studio [MGM] was hoping her new musical [*Torch Song*] would be a big hit. It was her very first movie in color, she still kept a great figure, and her leading man was Englishman Michael Wilding, better known domestically as Elizabeth Taylor's second husband. It was his big Tinseltown break. . . . Crawford played a rude, self-obsessed star—it wasn't what her fans wanted to see or believe. The movie bombed big-time."

—Joan Crawford biographer Bob Thomas

"Elizabeth Taylor stopped by the *Torch Song* set to visit her new husband, who was playing a blind pianist. . . . The male crew was happy to see Liz. Miss Crawford was not. She asked the studio to henceforth ban all visitors. . . . Joan Crawford was Old Hollywood—follow the rules, be a star twenty-four hours a day. Liz was New Hollywood—do your own thing, before anyone called it doing your own thing. The two women disliked each other. Understatement."

—columnist Lee Graham

"On June 21 [1952] Elizabeth announced she was pregnant. . . . Metro added two hours to her usual day's work, hoping to get her next film, *The Girl Who Had Everything*, in the can before her pregnancy began to show. . . . On August 1, 1952, after completing *The Girl*, Metro placed her on suspension because of her pregnancy instead of wishing her well and expressing their appreciation to her for the prosperity she'd brought to the studio ever since childhood."

—ET biographer Ellis Amburn

"When Elizabeth had two sons by Wilding her image shifted. She was now a mother. Not what the studio wanted; they wouldn't have had her playing mothers for years to come. But Elizabeth was adamant. She'd always wanted children. To her that was more important than the studio or her contract."

—MGM producer Joe Pasternak

"Elizabeth increasingly enjoyed being a mother. I think she decreasingly enjoyed being the wife of a quiet, nice older man. She made that amazing, for its time, public statement that they'd ended up more like brother and sister. Moving on to Mike Todd changed her image. By the time he died and she'd had another child, a daughter, and Elizabeth was latching on to Eddie Fisher, people forgot she'd ever been a mother."

—MGM star Esther Williams

"Monty Clift spent most of his time in New York. Elizabeth was usually working in Hollywood. When he came west to do a Hitchcock picture, Monty reunited with Elizabeth. He was at her home often, sometimes bringing along Rock Hudson. Elizabeth was very happy that Monty adored Michael [Wilding]. That was like a seal of approval for her."

—Monty intimate Jack Larson

"I've read that Clift hated his homosexuality. Untrue. He hated that public knowledge of it might so easily end his career. Elizabeth confirms this . . . she's appalled by people who can't distinguish homophobia from homosexuality. She cites Oscar Levant [pianist-actor-wit], who when an ignorant interviewer asked if Oscar was an 'unhappy Jew' answered, 'No. But I'm not too happy about anti-Semitism.'"

—bisexual poet-composer Rod McKuen

"Seems after the marriage to Hilton ended Elizabeth stopped taking her mother's counsel on matters matrimonial. She made her own decisions, and started choosing her own movie scripts. Sara was not happy . . . but eventually it has to happen, doesn't it?"

—columnist Dorothy Manners

"I'm friends with a closeted movie star who told me how protective Elizabeth is about Montgomery Clift. Like the time someone said he'd turned down *Sunset Boulevard* because of his older-woman lover Libby Holman, and the inevitable comparisons between his character with the character Norma Desmond. Liz chimed right in and said the two had been close friends and Holman was not Monty's lover. Whether or not that was partly out of jealousy, she was negating that irresistible urge most people and the news media have to de-gay someone by pretending they were lovers with an opposite-sex friend or associate."   —J. Russell King, deputy editor of, ironically, the *New York Times*

"It's been theorized that Clift would eventually have come out of the closet. Other than optimism, I don't know what that's based on. I don't know Elizabeth Taylor's opinion, but I doubt he would have. Rock Hudson never did; he only admitted to AIDS, which was then equated with being gay, though now we know three-quarters of PWA [People With AIDS] are heterosexual. Taylor did say Monty lamented that gay actors, in all their roles and with movies' constant invisibilizing of gay people, were always working 'in the service of heterosexuality.' So at least he had a raised social consciousness."
                              —actor Ron Vawter (*Philadelphia*)

"Miss Taylor had a crush on Montgomery Clift. Whether she was in love with him I don't know. I think everyone's heard that he was the unrequited love of her life. She evidently accepted the reality and, being a good friend, tried to introduce Monty to nice men who weren't necessarily showbiz types."
—Anne Revere, Clift's mother in *A Place in the Sun* (due to suddenly being blacklisted during the political witch hunts, most of Revere's scenes were cut from the movie)

"On the day of that horrific accident, Liz had to persuade Monty to come over to her and Michael's place that night. Monty was rather tired but Liz tempted him by telling him that another guest would be a hip young priest. And in passing, that somebody thought the priest was gay. Driving back home, Monty was alone. His pal Kevin McCarthy was in the car behind him, but Monty didn't have the priest with him. If he had, everybody would have known about it, because of the accident. Still, as Oscar Wilde once said, nothing looks so innocent as an indiscretion. Back then, people would have thought, oh, a *priest*, there couldn't be anything between *them*."
                                                    —ET's publicist John Springer

"During the whole time of the scandal about Eddie and Debbie,
I don't think I once read that Elizabeth Taylor was the mother of three
children. Instead, she was always the siren who lured Fisher away from
his apple-pie marriage. Show business is seldom about reality . . . like
they say, half the people in Hollywood are dying to be discovered,
while the other half are afraid they will be."
—film historian Doug McClelland

"Elizabeth helped save Monty's life after the accident. She scooped out the broken teeth that were plugging his throat and would have choked him. . . . When the press arrived, ready to photograph his bloodied, mangled face, she screamed that if they took one photo of Monty she would never let them photograph her again. Privately, Clift didn't see what Liz saw in Eddie Fisher, but he didn't reprimand her, and though Liz disliked Monty befriending Marilyn Monroe when they were in *The Misfits*, she didn't scold him. They never criticized each other. It was a platonic but unconditional love."
                                             —actress Nancy Walker, a close friend of Clift

"Eddie was my first love—and my first divorce. Eddie's best friend, producer Mike Todd, spent a lot of time with us while we were dating. Mike fell in love with Elizabeth Taylor. Eddie and I stood up for Mike and Elizabeth when they were married. When Mike was killed in a horrible plane crash I took care of their children while Eddie comforted Elizabeth. Then Eddie left our two small children and me for Elizabeth [in 1958]."

—Debbie Reynolds

"What turned Liz Taylor's image so sexy wasn't any one movie or her studio. It was her private life. Her mother was hoop-de-doo thrilled about the rich young men who came a-courting. You bet she made sure the columnists reported it! She wanted a prize catch for them—for Liz and herself by extension. She really shared her daughter's fame, just outside the spotlight. There were rich guys, but when the Hilton boy came along—wealth *and* a famous family name—basically the mother decided this was the one."

—producer David Lewis (*Raintree County*)

"He was a no-good bum, Nicky Hilton . . . living off his father's achievement. A boozer . . . and whispers about heroin. It took less than a few months of marriage for him to start his physical abuse. Elizabeth was devastated. So was her mother. At first she wanted to save the marriage, but she couldn't have her daughter black and blue. She did love her . . . so she grudgingly agreed to the divorce."

—MGM alumnus Ann Miller

"Even before Hopper chose to make it public, rumors about Michael Wilding must have reached Elizabeth's ears. On the other hand, why would she have fled a bisexual fiancé if he was nice and comforting? Her mother had married a nice gay man."

—MGM star June Allyson

"The marriage to Michael Wilding was made on the rebound. As a reaction against handsome, young, brash and American, violent Conrad Nicholas Hilton Jr. Wilding was older, he was English, polite, soft-spoken. . . . Hedda Hopper warned Liz in print not to marry him because he also liked men. Specifically, Stewart Granger. . . . Ironically, Hopper always shielded the homosexuality of her only son [William Hopper of *Perry Mason*]."
                                                    —Ken Ferguson, editor of British *Photoplay*

"Some have said Elizabeth loved her father so much that she was seeking a father figure in Michael Wilding. I don't think so. I think as she moved into her mid twenties she wanted more of a conventionally hot 'n heavy heterosexual relationship, and . . . along came Mike Todd."
                                                    —hairdresser Zak Taylor (no relation)

"It took many years for Elizabeth to reveal that Nicky Hilton had not only beaten her but caused her to have a miscarriage. In those days if a man beat a woman, many people presumed she'd somehow caused it. She confessed, 'I left him after having a baby kicked out of my stomach.'"
                                                    —ET biographer C. David Heymann

"Elizabeth made no public comment [about Hilton's death], and was far more grieved by the death of her secretary and trusted confidant Dick Hanley, who died in 1970 after having taken care of her like a father since the death of Mike Todd. She paid for a lavish funeral for Hanley and later held a wake at the Beverly Hills Hotel, sending a spectacular floral display with a card saying, 'I will love you always—Elizabeth.'"
                                                    —ET biographer Ellis Amburn

"When she met Mike Todd the fireworks began. He was a man of the world, self-made and self-named [born Avrom Goldbogen], highly successful and highly sexed. He began showering Liz with jewelry and sex . . . he unlocked her repressed libido, and from then on she became the biggest sex symbol outside Marilyn Monroe."   —Truman Capote

"Nicholas 'Nicky' Hilton died at 42 in 1969 of cardiac arrest surrounded by his sizeable gun collection. Not long before, a shrink had stated his intention of committing Hilton to the Menninger clinic."   —columnist Shirley Eder

"It's almost amusing in a parallel way. Marilyn was criticized for her sexuality on the screen. Elizabeth was criticized for her sexuality off the screen. Marilyn was often laughed at, often the butt of a joke. She was not perceived as a threat—except, in some quarters, to the nation's morals. Elizabeth Taylor was taken much more seriously—and was perceived as a threat . . . a homewrecker. She got much more heat than Marilyn ever did. Some people disliked Marilyn but few hated her. In her publicity heyday, Elizabeth was quite widely hated."   —Raymond Burr (*A Place in the Sun*)

"For a while there it seemed like Liz Taylor and Marilyn Monroe were competing in a famous-husbands sweepstakes. But Marilyn stopped at three husbands—two were already pretty famous when she married them. The only very famous one Liz married was Eddie Fisher. All her others became more famous after she married them."
—director Richard Brooks (*Cat on a Hot Tin Roof*)

"My sister [Joan Blondell] was a star who not only helped make Mike Todd well known, she also made him wealthy. Then he bankrupted her. He took her for some $3 million. . . . When they broke up, Joan said she felt lucky to have survived that marriage with just a broken arm and a nervous breakdown. . . . Todd was violent and a remorseless user."

—actress Gloria Blondell

"He did hit Elizabeth. More than once. Everybody later admitted that. What kept them together was the great sex and the lavish lifestyle, even if much of it was financed by her. He was an addictive gambler. . . . Elizabeth wasn't typically submissive, so she sort of enjoyed starting or helping start fights—and she particularly enjoyed making up after a fight."

—Gore Vidal

"I know she doesn't like being alone, and if the company is male, so much the better. She's an inveterate flirt. Elizabeth seems to enjoy drama in her life, even dangerous drama. Above all, I think she hates being bored or taken for granted."

—costar Susannah York (*X, Y and Zee; Zee and Company* in the UK)

"After one marriage to a drunken maniac and one to a nice but dull older man, Elizabeth was ready to be courted and taken to bed and taken care of. She liked the idea of a strong man taking care of her. Mike Todd was selfish but Elizabeth was infatuated. . . . She was also growing used to living in the public eye. . . . Mike was the first to recast Liz as a voluptuary, and she loved it."

—costar Paul Newman (*Cat on a Hot Tin Roof*)

"It was a pattern. Her first husband was aggressive, the second was passive. Third was aggressive, fourth was passive. The fifth was aggressive . . . you get the idea. Liz had a high opinion of herself, naturally, but it didn't preclude allowing a man to occasionally dominate or even rough her up."   —costar James Coco (*There Must Be a Pony*)

"Who knows but that she would sooner or later have left Mike Todd
except that she got pregnant and had a daughter and then
he died in an airplane crash?"
—costar and friend Laurence Harvey

"The private plane he crashed in was The Lucky Liz, and she certainly was. Elizabeth usually accompanied Todd whenever possible. He always wanted her around, to show her off. But she was bedridden with bronchitis, taking time off from [shooting] *Cat on a Hot Tin Roof*. So he flew to New York to be honored by the Friars Club as Showman of the Year or some such title. Elizabeth then suffered a bad case of survivor's guilt. But she did complete the picture, and she had everyone's sympathy. For a while. . . ."

—Tennessee Williams

"So far as I know, Eddie Fisher is straight. But he was definitely Mike Todd's boy. Call it Mike's charisma or . . . I don't know. Eddie was this big success in records and TV yet he jumped to do Mike's bidding, including babysitting Elizabeth Taylor when Mike was away. Mike kept pushing them together, and Eddie kept tagging along with Mike or Mike and Liz. All the while he was married to Debbie Reynolds—the grapevine said it was a loveless marriage but it did produce two kids. Then Mike was killed and Eddie knew he'd have been assigned to comfort Liz. So . . . he comforted her."   —Dean Martin

"Not everyone is one thing or the other. Many showbiz denizens go both ways. Before it was 'bisexual' it was 'double-gaited.' I don't doubt Eddie Fisher loved sex with women, if not women themselves. . . . Until Elizabeth Taylor, 'broads' were as disposable to Eddie as Kleenex. But Eddie's happy subservience to Mike Todd goes unexplained. Even before Liz, when Todd was unknown to the public and Eddie was a star, Eddie was so willing and eager to be around Mike, to do whatever he wanted . . . his nickname was 'Mike's boy.' Only because Eddie was such a success at the time, that nickname didn't damage him."

–Dick Haymes, another popular singer of the era

"Debbie Reynolds played the innocent wronged wife. She gave a press conference wearing her blonde pigtails and started wearing crucifixes. Eddie dumping her for bejeweled, glamorous Liz Taylor made Debbie into America's sweetheart. It made Taylor America's favorite target. She was vilified up and down . . . if her movies hadn't been hits Hollywood would have dumped her in a second. I have it on good authority Eddie had been planning to divorce Debbie until she announced she was pregnant."

–Tony Perkins

"I called Debbie and I told her bluntly, 'I'm with Elizabeth in New York and we're in love.' Debbie surprised me with her response. She was very calm. She said, 'We'll talk about it when you get home.' Talk about it! I'd just told her I was in love with another woman and she reacted as if I'd told her I'd be home a little late for dinner."

–Eddie Fisher

"About a year before Elizabeth Taylor happened to him, or at him, Eddie spoke to Debbie about divorce and they sort of made a plan. But he did nothing about it, maybe due to inertia and being content having a celebrity wife or guilt over being an almost absentee father."

—publicist Dale Olson

"Mike is dead and I'm alive."
—columnist Hedda Hopper, quoting ET out of context
and fanning the flames of hatred against her

"You know how much I loved Mike. I loved him more than my life. But Mike is dead now and I'm alive and the one person who would want me to try and live and be happy is Mike."

—what Elizabeth Taylor told Hedda Hopper about her relationship with Eddie Fisher

"Debbie enacted the jilted wife to perfection. She appeared in front of the press wearing a diaper pin in her blouse, to remind everyone she was a mother. Her public statement made out that she was shocked and surprised that I was in love with someone else, that we had an idyllic marriage. Never mind that we hadn't had sex in ages or had worked out details of a divorce some time before. As I read her public statement I began to hate her."

—Eddie Fisher

"The divorce made its three participants more famous than ever, and two of them richer. The one whose career languished was Fisher. He was beguiled, in love for the very first time. Foolishly, he neglected his career. He needn't have. Taylor was more blamed and hated than he was."

—ET biographer Alexander Walker

"Elizabeth and Eddie were receiving in the neighborhood of seven thousand angry letters a week. The senders varied . . . disgusted housewives, Ku Klux Klan officials, religious leaders. They received voodoo dolls with pins stuck in their genitals. . . . And other reactions too gross or obscene to mention." —columnist Mike Connolly

"Ratings for Fisher's show, cheerily sponsored by Chesterfield cigarettes, plummeted. Perversely, people were eager to see 'that scarlet woman,' Liz Taylor, seduce her way across the big screen. Her ratings, as it were, went up. Radio and TV were homey mediums. People didn't want their families exposed to 'immorality' in the living room. Whereas the movies were away from home, so people could leave the children behind and go watch and be thrilled." —film historian Douglas Whitney

"It was the most analyzed and reviled marriage since Edward VIII abdicated the throne to marry two-time American divorcee Wallis Simpson and became just the Duke of Windsor." —social sciences professor Dixie Rue

"Debbie continued grieving as publicly as possible. At times she told the columnists she didn't blame me, she blamed Elizabeth for stealing me away. Or she blamed Sinatra and Dean Martin for corrupting me with their drinking and gambling. She said she would welcome me back, explaining how lucky I was 'to be loved by two women.' And she posed forlornly for various magazines, including one photo with the kids and a dog, captioned, 'Can't Daddy be with us all the time?' Meanwhile, she continued to work. . . . Within a year her annual income had soared from less than $75,000 to almost $1 million." —Eddie Fisher

"Eddie told me if he hadn't met Elizabeth Taylor he would still and certainly have left Debbie Reynolds. His misfortune was not leaving her sooner, so that the nation believed he acted viciously and was destroying a happy marriage. It was the beginning of his end, while it was simply onward and upward for Liz."
—columnist Jack O'Brian

"I do mind that it's forgotten, but it is still a historical fact that I earned $1 million a year on TV before Elizabeth signed her million-dollar contract for *Cleopatra*. . . . That was in 1953 and ten times what President Eisenhower was earning. The most expensive cars were $3,000. Houses were $7,000."
—Eddie Fisher

"I must admit Elizabeth seemed to enjoy the drama that attended their affair—apart from the times when the press grew intrusive and the crowds grew large and ominous. Just to leave the house, she and Eddie had to lie flat in the backseat of a car I or another friend was driving."
—Roddy McDowall

"The only thing that marred our honeymoon was a phone call from Louella Parsons, who asked, 'Did you know that your son just had a hernia operation in Palm Springs?' When I told her I knew nothing about it she admitted, 'Debbie called me to try to find you.' Debbie had to call one of the most famous gossip columnists in the world to find me? How about reading any newspaper in America? How about calling my agent or my business manager or even my mother? Instead she called a newspaper columnist. And by the time she placed that call the operation was done and Todd was perfectly fine."
—Eddie Fisher, whose son was named after Mike Todd

"The smear campaign against Taylor continued until her emotional and health problems resulted in a near-coma and her almost dying . . . when they had to perform the emergency tracheotomy in London. So America made peace with its biggest star. Until, on the set of *Cleopatra* in Rome, she enticed Richard Burton away from his wife and children. All over again, and more so, it was time to loathe Liz."

—producer Daniel Melnick (*That's Entertainment!*)

"I liked Liz Taylor until she kept jumping around from husband to husband. It's good exercise, but is that dignified?"   —Morey Amsterdam (*The Dick Van Dyke Show*)

"The thing that keeps Elizabeth Taylor from becoming a joke is her wealth and box office and her barely contained anger. And her dignity. I guess that's really four things."

—scriptwriter Marguerite Roberts, who during the McCarthy era refused to name names for MGM and was blacklisted, her credit removed from *Ivanhoe*, costarring ET

"I've heard Miss Taylor has breeding and good manners. But the two times I've come across her in the flesh, she rather scared me. She's not someone you go up to and say, 'Hi, I'm a fan,' or even, 'Hello, how are you?' I guess you *could* say hello. I'm not sure what her response would be, and I wouldn't want to gamble and find out."

—stage set designer Ben Edwards

"I've seen at least one man get close to her and stare—because visually she's mighty impressive—then become tongue-tied and go all goofy-smiling."
—columnist Dorothy Kilgallen

"Anyone who is against me will look like a rat—unless I run off with Eddie Fisher."

—presidential widow Jacqueline Kennedy, to a reporter

"She's tiny, but she's huge. I mean the impression . . . or impact. I wouldn't dare approach and ask her for her autograph." —actress Peggy Cass (*Auntie Mame*)

"When did she stop being a nice English girl and become a Hollywood tramp?"

—columnist Sheilah Graham to author Calder Willingham

"This country must be running out of eligible Christian gentlemen if she has to go marrying two Jewish men in a row." —actor and political witch-hunter Ward Bond

"It was the marriage to Mike Todd that spoiled her. She was fairly normal before him—spoiled by her mother, sure. But Todd corrupted her . . . sex, jewelry, cleavage, greed, the high life. He made a big difference in her lifestyle." —screenwriter Jay Presson Allen

"Elizabeth Taylor and Richard Burton perfectly encapsulate the decadence of Hollywood stardom. The most materialistic, show-offy, self-satisfied, acquisitive, camera-ready, attention-needy couple the silver screen has yet produced. . . . Hollywood corrupted them and they corrupt each other." —novelist Henry Farrell

"Eddie Fisher changed her image for keeps. From the moment he left Debbie Reynolds for Liz, she became best known for marriages and more marriages. She became a serial semi-monogamist." —actress June Haver (wife of Fred MacMurray)

"She has been gifted with beauty she didn't earn . . . and has misused. She throws it at men and ensnares them. She ruins lives and marriages. She's what used to be called a vamp . . . a destructive siren."
—actor Adolphe Menjou

"And now she legitimizes her immoral affair with Richard Burton, divorced father of two, by marrying him. As if it was perfectly legitimate all along. Well, it wasn't and it is not!"
—Southern evangelist Horace Rufus

"She does not respect marriage. It's a mere game to her, the culmination of each romantic indulgence. Now that she is become Mrs. Richard Burton the world smiles and oohs and ahs. Mark my words, there will be a divorce. Can you possibly believe otherwise?"
—Los Angeles mayor Sam Yorty

"Richard Burton once listed his wife's qualities for me . . . apart from those to do with beauty and sex he said she was shy, arrogant, witty, strong-willed, loyal, talented, impatient of phonies, tolerant of his excessive drinking, exciting to be around, terrible to be apart from, and that she still loved him."   —Ingrid Sischy, editor of *Interview* magazine

"If I had known that first night together how our love was going to help destroy my career and, for a time, my life, if I had known how much pain my love for Elizabeth was going to bring me, I still wouldn't have hesitated. Whatever happened between us, it was worth it."
—Eddie Fisher

"Elizabeth Taylor's one and only non-tempestuous, even-keeled marriage was the one to Michael Wilding. The irony is that although bisexual, he fathered her two sons—if that's even ironical. We tend to think in stereotypes."
                                                                —British actress Martita Hunt

"Hedda Hopper was a fascist who lambasted President Kennedy for helping to end the witch hunts that targeted Hollywood after the Republicans took Congress in 1947. She was virulently anti-gay . . . tried to 'out' Cary Grant, but he was too big a star. After she warned Elizabeth Taylor in print not to marry Michael Wilding, he confessed to Elizabeth that his first wife had proposed to *him*. Elizabeth married him anyway."
—ET's *Jane Eyre* costar Peggy Ann Garner

"Though Richard Burton was the second grand passion of Elizabeth Taylor's life, he was homoerotically inclined enough to have had sex with Laurence Olivier."
                                                                —ET biographer Ellis Amburn

"What's sort of sad is all the post-Burton men Elizabeth Taylor got engaged to . . . nearly married. Each gave her a flashy engagement ring. I think they were all straight, I know they were all rich—or she wouldn't have given them the time of *date*. Being rich, they weren't gold-diggers, but they were publicity-diggers. And Liz loved, she thrived on, the publicity surrounding her romances and engagements and the re-marriage speculation and then the broken engagements. No, it *was* sad, not just sort of."
                                                                —Las Vegas costume designer Lloyd Lambert

"My opinion is only that, but Elizabeth shares it. I don't believe Richard had an ongoing sexual relationship with Philip Burton. Burton kept Richard, financially and otherwise, but I think Richard was too in awe of him to become and remain lovers. We do believe Richard had a few affairs with actors, including Olivier and possibly my father [Emlyn Williams], who was bisexual in his youth."

—friend Brook Williams, who had bit roles in several Richard Burton films

"Elizabeth told me that every single man she's been married or engaged to or dated has been, overall, a positive experience. Except Eddie Fisher."
—Dominick Dunne, producer of ET's film *Ash Wednesday*

"Liz hit the roof when Fisher published *Been There, Done That*. It paints him as a clever and talented fool for love who's had every woman in Hollywood. . . . At least he depicted Liz as the love of his life, that is, until his final wife, who's rich and Chinese. He didn't tell how he tried to blackmail Taylor over money when they were divorcing over Richard Burton. Fisher made several women unhappy with that book, not just telling lies but also telling the truth, like blow jobs from a famous redheaded actress who's still alive and married now. That book killed any residual sympathy anyone in showbiz had for Fisher. But he doesn't need them, not with a rich and contented non-show-business wife."

—director Garry Marshall

"Elizabeth Taylor banned all mention of Eddie Fisher's memoir, which she blasted as semi fiction. She had a brief laugh when a friend said there was enough baloney in it to open a deli."

—British talk show host David Frost

"Sturm has remarried Drang, and all is right with the world."
—the *Boston Globe*, on the Taylor-Burton remarriage in 1975

"For their second wedding, Elizabeth Taylor and Richard Burton went to Botswana, Africa, where they could be alone. Except for a hundred or so photographers and press. And the cheetah the remarried couple posed with. Of course Dick bought Liz a little commemorative gift: a one-million-dollar pink-diamond ring."
—former agent Robert Hussong

"Some people outside London and Hollywood were genuinely shocked when Liz and Dick divorced in 1974. But even in London and Hollywood we were shocked when they remarried the following year. Half of us thought it was for publicity, half thought it was for love. Few of us thought it would last." —British director Bryan Forbes

"Her first marriage to Burton ran about ten years. The second was ten months. Bets were on that if they re-remarried, it would last ten weeks. Or ten days."
—comedian Rodney Dangerfield

"I was astounded when Elizabeth and Richard chose to do Noël Coward's *Private Lives*. Elizabeth's stage bow was in *The Little Foxes*, of which I did the screen version. It was a good and brave choice, and she did a fine job. But this! She and Richard had divorced. They had undertaken marriages to new people—marriages that were on the rocks—and now they were re-teaming. But that's exactly what *Private Lives* is about! So really it became *Public Lives*. Or *Private Lives on Exhibit*. No wonder all the tickets sold!"
—Bette Davis

"Before and after marriage #2 to Richard Burton, Elizabeth was involved with Henry Wynberg. She met him because she was going around with, and possibly dating, Christopher Lawford [then age eighteen], son of Peter Lawford, who for some years was President Kennedy's brother-in-law. Peter was rattled when an interviewer asked if his son was having an affair with Elizabeth Taylor. He denied it but immediately introduced her to a man in her own age bracket—a used-car salesman. To Peter's delight, Liz and Henry got along famously."
—Hollywood hostess Jean Howard

"Poor Henry Wynberg . . . the most belittled man in Elizabeth's life besides Eddie Fisher. His profession . . . and he'd been convicted and fined for setting back automobile odometers. But he did comfort Elizabeth during the time when she'd re-lost Richard and was having more health problems. Henry was Dutch-born and had a soft voice. He had a hairy chest he liked to show off. Elizabeth made sure their romance was well publicized and photographed . . . to show Richard and the world that she could do without Richard, even though she didn't want to."
—William F. Dufty, who ghostwrote about forty books, including Billie Holiday's *Lady Sings the Blues*

"It was Henry Wynberg who planted the idea in Elizabeth's head about creating her own perfume so she could make a fortune and not have to continue acting."
—Natalie Wood

"You can't keep clapping a couple of sticks of dynamite together without expecting them to blow up."
—Richard Burton, about himself and ET

"It was like a yo-yo. She'd reconcile with Richard, they'd quarrel, she'd go back to Henry. No big quarrels with Henry, but then Richard would show up, she'd return to Richard, then they'd bust up, then back to Henry. Henry made Richard jealous. . . . Henry was her cat's paw. Perhaps he didn't really mind. Years afterward, he spoke well of Liz."

—columnist Lloyd Shearer

"When Elizabeth made the final break with Wynberg it was in front of Richard in Switzerland. She told him they were through, that she was back with Richard, they were going to re-marry, and she gifted Henry with $50,000 and a gold watch—as if she'd retired him."

—press agent Beebe Kline

"Of course she was beside herself when Burton married the blonde [Susan Hunt in 1976]. He hardly waited three weeks after divorcing Elizabeth before remarrying. To some extent, Elizabeth was waiting for him to divorce . . . but he stayed married. It lasted till 1982 and the next year he married his female assistant, an Australian [Sally Hay]. They lasted until he died of a stroke a few years later. It was very rough on Elizabeth . . . it took a long time for it to become crystal clear that he wasn't going to return to her."

—costar Hermione Gingold (*A Little Night Music*)

"Suzy Hunt banished all of Richard's entourage except Brook Williams. They were a boozy lot, and she wanted a sober husband, which is nearly always preferable."

—actress Sian Phillips, ex-wife of alcoholic Peter O'Toole

"I think Suzy Hunt provided a very important gift to him.
She made him able to leave Elizabeth."
—Richard Burton's daughter Kate Burton

"The 1980s was an odd decade for Liz Taylor in that she spent most of it unmarried. Not that she didn't have male company." —fashion designer Isaac Mizrahi

"Nineteen-eighty-four has proven a busy social year for Elizabeth Taylor. . . . She returned Victor Luna's engagement ring, she dated Carl Bernstein of Woodward and Bernstein fame [authors of *All the President's Men*], and she announced her engagement to businessman Dennis Stein." —writer Ingrid Sischy

"Elizabeth would have married Dennis Stein, a flashy Brooklynite who sold blue jeans and promoted himself. After they dated in 1984, Elizabeth accepted his twenty-carat sapphire engagement ring and began planning her wedding gown. She even took him to her Swiss chalet in Gstaad for the holidays. But by early '85 it was over. The sole cause we know of is he talked to the press, praising her like a fan even though she'd warned him, 'No interviews.' But he talked . . . and she walked." —columnist Richard Gully

"Elizabeth had relapses . . . she was no stranger to the Betty Ford Clinic where she met the Larry guy who operated an off-road dirt compactor, whatever that is. Anyway, he was dazzled by who she was and she beheld this young, pudgy blond, they flirted and talked and whatever, and maybe she saw it as a publicity opportunity and/or a possible romance and, realistically, probably her last chance at matrimony." —publicist Andrea Jaffe

"Twice in her life Elizabeth proposed marriage to a man. First to Michael [Wilding], twenty years her senior. Second to her final husband [Larry Fortensky], who was twenty-one years her junior. . . . At Betty Ford people are told to not become involved until a year after they meet, but Elizabeth ignored the rule. . . . It was highly sexual, but she didn't *know* the man. They married much too soon. It was more of a co-dependency between two ex-alcoholics than a stable marriage."   —star and ET friend Jean Simmons

"But why did she have to marry him? I appreciate what the construction workers do. And some are handsome, some I suppose make a good lover. But what could she and he have in common? Except their addiction and being in the same recovery program. What else?"   —Spanish movie star Sara Montiel

"It was a very gay wedding when Liz tied the knot [in 1991] with Larry Fortensky. Best man was Michael Jackson, whose fake date was Brooke Shields. Guests included Barry Diller *with* Diane von Furstenberg, Merv Griffin *with* Eva Gabor . . . hairdressers Sydney Guilaroff and Jose Eber without 'dates' . . . Roddy McDowall, Liz Smith, and the wedding gown was by Valentino."   —*Entertainment Tonight* writer Wayne Warga

"[Larry] beat me like crazy. He blackened my eyes, kicked me and pounded my head with his fists. And when he hit me, he didn't hold back, even though I'm just 5′6″ and weigh 132 pounds while he's 6′2″ and weighs over 200 pounds. . . . He drank and popped pills all day long. He smoked pot. He was drunk every day. And he's a mean drunk."
—Kelly Matzinger, Fortensky's second wife (ET was his third)

"One time, Elizabeth took off her super-expensive diamond ring to wash her hands in the john at Hamburger Hamlet in Los Angeles. When she got home she realized she'd left it behind. Larry ranted and raved . . . she yelled back that it was her goddamn ring and she'd just call the restaurant and ask them to deliver it. Which they did."

—columnist Arlene Walsh

"She accustomed Fortensky to a lavish lifestyle. The money Elizabeth gave him ruined him. He was disoriented and became greedy, angry, and suspicious. . . . He didn't treat ordinary people well, including the servants. Elizabeth wondered if she'd done right, bringing him into her house. He wouldn't adjust and did not belong. Yet she couldn't end it too soon. She felt sorry for him but cringed at the upcoming public ridicule. If you ask me, the last two husbands made Eddie Fisher look viable."

—Roddy McDowall

"One day, she walked into the kitchen and happened upon Larry berating one of her female employees. He raised his hand to her. Would he have hit her? Elizabeth was alarmed enough by the possibility to immediately step between them. 'Larry, I don't know how you treat your construction crews, but you will not behave this way to my staff,' she said angrily. 'They are more than employees. They're my family.' Larry stormed off and shut himself up in his bedroom, where he slept for three days straight."

—ET biographer J. Randy Taraborrelli

"In 1995 Liz told Larry he would have to go. He hated to give up, and took Liz to a marriage counselor. No use. When they separated, she gave the press the fiction that it was only a trial separation and she hoped they could get together again. . . . When Liz moved to divorce Larry she was flabbergasted that he was suing her for $5 million and trying to invalidate their prenuptial agreement. In the end, she settled about $1 million on him and publicly wished him well. In 1996 she was officially rid of him."

—publicist Ronni Chasen

"At forty-seven, Larry Fortensky was still despairing over his divorce from Elizabeth, spending all day lolling around his condo in San Juan Capistrano, California, or drinking and starting brawls at the Swallow Inn. One friend felt that many people around town wanted to get rid of him. On January 28, 1999, he either fell or was pushed headfirst down a seven-foot circular staircase in his home, landing on his head and sustaining a broken bone in his neck, several splintered discs in his spine, and massive head injuries so serious he might never walk, talk, or move again. His alcohol level at the time was .265."

—ET biographer Ellis Amburn

"Elizabeth once confided, cold sober, that you can't always fry the fish you want to fry. She meant about who all she married . . . said that several of the men she'd like to have married weren't interested in women. She added, without any segue, that Richard Burton was the one worth quarreling with. She said he thought she drank too much and she knew that he did drink too much, but when love happens between two people you have to follow it through and not listen to what others think. All Richard's Welsh and English friends had warned him not to 'go Hollywood,' to stick to the artistic path. But love intervened."

—Truman Capote

"According to Monty, Richard confessed to Elizabeth after they were married that while climbing his way up the stage ladder in England he'd agreed to the advances of Laurence Olivier and John Gielgud. Elizabeth wasn't shocked. She replied that Hollywood had a casting couch too, only more blatant. What she did ask Richard was whether that was all in his past. . . . I wonder if she'd have minded more an infidelity with a woman or with a man?"   —Montgomery Clift companion and former actor Jack Larson

"You wouldn't think someone like Liz Taylor would ever have experienced the casting couch, and it's very possible she didn't. If she had, it would probably have been during that awkward period between child star and grown star. Those guys in Hollywood, they don't care if a female's underage. Gratification and status and box office—that's everything they care about."   —Roseanne Barr

"When they met in 1984 and became chums, Michael Jackson was twenty-six and Elizabeth was fifty-two. What did they have in common besides being famous as kids? Here's a big clue: Liz was worth about $75 million and Michael was worth about $300 million. She loved gifts and he loved, or needed, respectability and favorable publicity. Greed and need. Nuff said?"
—Ray Stricklyn, actor and friend of Tennessee Williams

"Successful as she is, Elizabeth still feels the need of a man to validate her. Someone to pay her attention and romance her, seemingly or actually . . . to make her feel and look desired. She isn't as strong as the impression she gives, except physically. . . . Acting is almost a sideline for her. Her personal life comes first." —actor and boyfriend Rod Steiger

"Jackson paraded several actresses as girlfriends, who later admitted the truth, like Tatum O'Neal, Brooke Shields, etc. When Michael met Liz Taylor he even pretended it was a romantic thing with her! Who in their right mind would believe that? But in one of those books Liberace 'authored' he claimed his first sexual experience was with an older female named Miss Bea Haven. Fans, which is short for fanatics, often believe just what they want to believe, appearances and facts be damned."

—screenwriter Jeffrey Boam (*Indiana Jones and the Last Crusade*)

"Elizabeth says she knew she wanted to be a mother while she was a child in England. Later, she someday wanted to have a husband . . . she assumed one husband, total. Acting didn't enter her head. It entered her mother's head, for Elizabeth, after they left England. If not for World War II, today she'd probably be a good-looking grandmother living in the English countryside."

—British writer Gavin Lambert

"Two gay men changed Elizabeth's life. First was Victor Cazalet, a wealthy, unmarried Member of Parliament who for cover was in the Conservative Party. He and Francis were a discreet pair, but when [WWII] broke out Cazalet was instrumental in enabling Francis and Sara and their children to move to the United States. Second was Northern Irish actor Stephen Boyd—*Cleopatra*'s first Mark Anthony until the production was delayed, then moved to Rome. When it resumed, Boyd had left and was replaced by a Welsh actor named Richard Burton."

—ET's secretary Roger Wall

CHAPTER 4
The Woman

"She certainly followed her heart. Regardless where it took her."　　　—Jerry Seinfeld

"If love is blind, Elizabeth Taylor has gone blind at least a dozen times. Temporarily . . . she's pretty clear-eyed. She doesn't let an affair or marriage cut her off from the rest of her life."　　　—Jack Haley Jr., director (*That's Entertainment!*)

"The public thinks of Miss Taylor as just an actress and a very glamorous wife. There's much more to her than that."　　　—ET's publicist Chen Sam

"Like the little girl in the fairy tale, Elizabeth is in love with love.
She's happiest when she is in love."
—mother Sara Taylor

"Being a mother is a vital part of Elizabeth's life. She is a devoted mother, and has been for a long time. . . . Her husbands are also a big part of Elizabeth's life, but only part of her life. Of course, when photographs and newsreels show only her and her latest husband, that's all the world sees and knows about."

—friend since childhood Roddy McDowall

"When we did *Lassie, Come Home*, Elizabeth said she wanted a Collie of her own. Or a Collie puppy and a baby. I teased her, I asked which would she choose, a puppy or a baby? She said a puppy because it was easier to take care of and quieter than a baby, which her mother probably wouldn't let her have."
—Roddy McDowall, four years ET's senior

"We'd both gone to the MGM high school, which was one room with a tiny bathroom where Elizabeth would hide to avoid lessons. The teacher would wait about fifteen minutes and then knock on the door and ask if Elizabeth was all right. Elizabeth always had some excuse for why she needed to be locked in the little girls' room. She was growing from a beautiful child into a beautiful woman who didn't think she needed to spend time on lessons. I was seventeen and still planned to be a gym teacher."
—Debbie Reynolds

"Like many pretty child actresses, Elizabeth Taylor didn't assume she'd be acting forever. Most girls considered the option of giving up acting for a good, meaning moneyed, marriage. . . . By sixteen or seventeen many of them had had their fill of acting, which was usually their mother's idea anyway."   —"plain jane" ex–child star Jane Withers

"One scandal Elizabeth didn't engage in was having a child out of wedlock. Maybe she remembered how doing so cost Ingrid Bergman her Hollywood career—she had to go to Europe to find work. . . . It's not surprising both her daughters avoided the acting profession. How could they hope to compete with Elizabeth Taylor?"
—Doris Roberts (*Everybody Loves Raymond*)

"Elizabeth doesn't necessarily approve of it but she doesn't judge actresses who've had a love child, like Vanessa Redgrave. If she judges Redgrave, it's for her anti-Israel stance and hypocrisy. . . . Elizabeth would only have a child in wedlock, thinking of her child's comfort and its future. So-called illegitimacy was a most significant stigma in the past."
—producer Renée Valente

"The public almost never sees Elizabeth Taylor's children. That is by design."
—photographer Kenn Duncan

"When one of her sons had a daughter out of wedlock, Elizabeth was not pleased. But it was the 1970s, things had changed and judgments softened. She adjusted to the situation. She's never been exactly a prig."   —actress Constance Ford (*A Summer Place*)

"Few people outside Hollywood are aware that Liz Taylor is a shrewd businesswoman and a tough negotiator. It's not new to her, like with Lucille Ball when she took over RKO studios. When a girl becomes her family's main and then sole financial support, as with Liz or Shirley Temple, she soon becomes aware of her fiscal responsibilities and opportunities. Regardless of her public image."   —film historian Doug McClelland

"I've been compared more often with Marilyn [Monroe], I guess because of being blonde. In reality I identify more with Liz Taylor. She's a strong personality whose personal and professional choices got her a lot of flak. But she's outlasted all that, hasn't she?"
—Madonna

"There's almost nothing an actress can do today to ruin her career, and few things for an actor. During Elizabeth Taylor's long career there were many things . . . many times her career could have just stopped. . . . She quit acting only when she decided to, when her health got worse."
—Neil Patrick Harris

"If she'd been that concerned about her career, Elizabeth Taylor wouldn't have taken so many chances. Each scandal threatened her ability to find work. She wasn't some careful career strategist."
—Hugh Grant

"I don't think she gives or gave a flying fig what the masses think. It's refreshing that Miss Taylor did her own thing back when people and especially stars were so very careful about what everyone else thought."
—costar Hermione Gingold (*A Little Night Music*)

"Liz Taylor didn't back down. Didn't apologize. Many people admired that. . . . Look at when Jane Fonda apologized for being photographed in Hanoi. The same people hating her for it still hated her after the apology. To my knowledge, Liz never apologized for anything. Not publicly."
—Walter Matthau

"Elizabeth did apologize to me and we became friends. We had a lot in common—we couldn't stand Eddie Fisher! . . . Eventually we even worked together [in the telefilm *These Old Broads*, cowritten by daughter Carrie Fisher]. . . . I was one of the last people Elizabeth telephoned before she died."
—Debbie Reynolds

"Taylor stood next to Sybil Burton Christopher [at a memorial for Roddy McDowall] and to my surprise embraced her. The tabloids had written at length about the two women's enmity, which began when Richard left Sybil for Elizabeth. Their reconciliation was apparently not salacious enough to report."   —ET biographer M. G. Lord

"She touched on the topic of her career ending. It didn't much concern her. She'd been in the movies since childhood and could walk away from it. Inasfar as money, there were savings in the bank and Elizabeth knew there would always be rich men willing to gift her with diamonds and funds so long as her looks lasted, and beyond that, so long as her fame lasted."   —producer Renée Valente

"In a good mood, Elizabeth told a fan who was staring at her from about ten feet away, 'I look younger if you squint.'"
—ET's secretary Roger Wall

"There was a stage project I tried several times to launch. It did not eventuate. Much later, in conversation with Elizabeth Taylor I told her about it. She insisted that to get what you want all you have to do is scream and yell and keep yelling until you get it. At first I thought she was joking. I doubt it would have worked for me."
—actress Lilli Palmer, a former wife of Rex Harrison

"Sometimes she's very inconsistent. She's ruled by caprices . . . she's so volatile, her moods change quickly. If she contradicts herself, she has no qualms about it, that's just her nature. Elizabeth isn't one to excuse herself."
—Milton Katselas, who directed ET in the play *Private Lives*

"Elizabeth doted on Dr. Arnold Klein, who she said literally saved her life. He became Michael Jackson's dermatologist. After Jackson died and Klein publicly admitted Michael was gay, Elizabeth turned on him, though she herself urged [costume designer] Nolan Miller several times to come out of the closet."

—novelist and Hollywood insider Jackie Collins

"Her sympathies are liberal but her inclination is without question pretty materialistic."
—costar Peter Ustinov (*The Comedians*)

"Making her happy was what made me happy. I couldn't buy enough for her. I guess that was the Mike [Todd] in me. I gave her jewels and clothes and furs. How many jewels were enough for the woman I loved? Just a few more than she had. For her twenty-seventh birthday I had a handbag made studded with twenty-seven diamonds spelling out LIZ. I never called her Liz, but even I couldn't afford ELIZABETH."

—fourth husband Eddie Fisher

"After *Cleopatra* Richard Burton's salary zoomed. He still didn't earn as much as she, but he looked to be spending more than her. When diamonds were purchased, he did the purchasing, she did the receiving. Whether in return she contributed more to their living expenses, only their accountant knows for sure."

—costar Julie Harris (*Reflections in a Golden Eye*)

"In effect, Burton was buying her all those jewels with money she enabled him to earn. She could easily have afforded to buy her own. I guess it made him feel more macho. He was the big spender who made sure everybody knew it. One of those outsized diamonds he bought Liz, he posed with it hanging on his forehead. Burton made several movies in Hollywood but he didn't become a Hollywood star until Liz."

—talk show host Skip E. Lowe

"Aaron Frosch once said that between us we created as much business as a small African state."

—from Richard Burton's diary entry for October 24, 1968
(regarding his lawyer's comment on the Taylor-Burton earnings)

"Even if it was more or less an illusion, Elizabeth Taylor enjoyed the idea and gesture of a man giving her expensive jewelry. To her, it was a proof of love. Not that one magnificent piece of jewelry was enough proof."
—former MGM star Esther Williams

"The Peregrina Pearl only cost $37,000 but its provenance gave Burton international publicity. Philip, king of Spain, gave it to Mary Tudor—elder daughter of Henry VIII and half sister of Elizabeth I—in 1554. As a Catholic monarch she was nicknamed Bloody Mary by English Protestants. Richard loved the history and romance of La Peregrina [meaning The Pilgrim] and wanted to write a book about it. But it cost him approximately $100,000 more to buy Elizabeth a pearl-ruby-and-diamond necklace to hang it from."

—diamond merchant S. A. Rabinowitz

"When Richard Burton bought Elizabeth the Krupp diamond [33.19 carats, $305,000] I thought it was grandstanding. But Elizabeth lightened the mood. The previous owner was the widow of Baron Krupp, a convicted Nazi arms manufacturer. So Elizabeth told the press, 'It's fitting that a nice little Jewish girl like me has ended up with the baron's rock.' Don't you love it?"

—Lauren Bacall

"My great-grandfather was a Polish Jew named Jan Ysar, and that was the family name until they changed it to Jenkins. It's true, I'm one-eighth Jewish. Elizabeth hasn't a drop of Jewish blood. I've told her so. It makes her furious."

—Richard Burton

"Is that the famous diamond? It's so large. How very vulgar. . . .
Would you mind if I tried it on?"
–Princess Margaret to ET about the Krupp diamond

"Sometime in the late '60s Richard was in a very foul mood. They were in a restaurant in Italy and Elizabeth reached across the table to him. What he said really cost him: 'I do not wish to touch your hands. They are large and ugly and red and masculine.' Elizabeth was stunned. But she found a way for him to make up. There was a certain diamond ring she fancied. She told Richard, 'It will make my ugly, big hands look smaller and less ugly. . . .'"

—Sam Kashner, coauthor of the ET-RB biography *Furious Love*

"Lloyds' insurance guidelines were strict. The diamond had to be stored in a vault, armed security men had to accompany Elizabeth Taylor whenever she wore it, and she could only wear it in public for thirty days out of the year. Small wonder she had a copy made for under $3,000 and sometimes wore it out instead."

—Sarah Petit, a *Newsweek* editor

"What became known as the Taylor-Burton diamond, one of the world's largest at 69.42 carats, came up for auction in 1969. Richard Burton authorized his solicitor [lawyer] to telephone-bid up to $1 million. Cartier barely outbid him. Aristotle Onassis had wanted it for Jackie but not for over $700,000. The Taylors were despondent, so Richard's man approached Cartier directly. He was willing to pay up to $2 million . . . he got it for about $1.1 million. But it was too large for a ring, so it became the pear-shaped centerpiece of an $80,000 diamond necklace, insured by Lloyds of London."   —jeweler Schuyler Dann

"Three men carrying identical briefcases, only one of which contained the Taylor-Burton diamond, left New York by plane for Nice, escorted by an armed security guard. From Nice they crossed the frontier of Monaco, where the *Kalizma* was berthed in Monte Carlo harbor. Once there, another armed guard, complete with submachine gun, was hired to protect the jewel."   —Nancy Schoenberger, coauthor of *Furious Love*

"Richard and Elizabeth named their yacht the *Kalizma* after their daughters . . . his daughter Kate, her daughter Liza, and their adopted daughter Maria. But it left out his daughter Jessica, who was mentally challenged and had to be institutionalized."
                                        —Ron Berkeley, Richard Burton's hairdresser

"Not many people know that Elizabeth adopted a little German girl, then paid for over 20 operations to correct her hip deformity. She adopted Maria with Eddie Fisher. When they divorced Elizabeth asked for and received custody—he didn't care. So she gave Maria her next husband's name . . . Maria Burton. Her fourth child."
                    —Fay Kanin, AMPAS (Academy of Motion Picture Arts and Sciences)
                                        president and screenwriter (ET's *Rhapsody*)

"Ms. Taylor is a dedicated and generous godmother . . . to the adopted son of her friend [and interior designer] Waldo Fernandez and his life partner. Elizabeth Taylor has inveighed against those remaining states whose laws prohibit gay or lesbian couples from adopting. It's a topic that, properly so, riles her."   —actress-activist Jane Lynch (*Glee*)

"Elizabeth placed her jewels in red leather boxes, eventually amassing an $8 million collection. Her total wealth at the time [circa 1968], according to Richard, was $20 million; his, $10 million. They could well afford to be generous to their staff of thirty."
—*The Most Beautiful Woman in the World* author Ellis Amburn

"The people who worked for them worshipped them."

—writer-producer Dominick Dunne

"She has a tendency to treat her male escorts, husbands too, like assistants or even servants. When they stand up to her she often stands right back up to them, like they're being impertinent. But, after all, she is Hollywood royalty."

—talk show host Mike Douglas

"Elizabeth Taylor grew up spoiled but her parents must have taught her manners. Unlike so many Americans, she often uses 'please' and 'thank you,' and she performs good table manners. . . . It has been remarked that she behaves better when alone. But she seldom is—there's almost always a man at her side."   —British actress Coral Browne

"She liked me, which was unusual. Apparently she didn't tolerate women well, preferring to hold court with men—gay, straight, both, didn't matter as long as they had balls. The reason she was okay with me? I had balls too. One day we were in the kitchen and she said, 'Linda, get me some orange juice.' I said, 'Get your own orange juice.' She started laughing that great laugh of hers, just like in the movies."　　—Linda Gray (*Dallas*)

"She has an impish, even perverse sense of humor. I remember one soiree where an attractive actress in her sixties was pretending that someday she'd probably be forced to have plastic surgery. Already *had*. . . . Her next topic was aging. During all this Elizabeth had been talking to some man who got up to refill her drink. So the first thing Liz hears is the actress saying, 'I shudder to even *think* about turning sixty.' For a second, no one says anything. Then Liz sweetly asks, 'Really? What happened then?'"　　—agent Dick Clayton

"She loves gossip, and when she dishes it out she sounds just like a fan. Loves to hear it, but prefers true gossip, not just idle rumors. Most likely because there were and are so many rumors about her."
—Sir John Gielgud

"At one dinner party, during dessert, an inebriated Lithuanian caught all ears when he asked Richard if the rumor was true that he'd slept with all his leading ladies except Julie Andrews? Burton said nothing, just grinned sheepishly. So Elizabeth put in, 'It's too true, and Miss Julie will never know what she missed. Although a few leading men do, don't they, luv?' Dick retained his grin and lowered his eyelids, symbolically dropping the curtain on the subject. They really were a fabulous pair."　　—Leonard Bernstein

"I costarred with Richard [in *Sea Wife*] before Elizabeth did. He's a great one for flirting and joking. However, his reputation for lechery is partly public relations. Everyone in this business occasionally exaggerates or prevaricates about whom they've *had*, but it's all in the name of business . . . it sells books, it makes a star more interesting, gets you invited onto chat shows, and somehow it's more important for a man."   —Joan Collins

"Miss Taylor loves to laugh. If a party has been full of laughs, she considers it a success and it was worth attending. Dull, serious affairs and people bore her to death."

—ET's publicist Chen Sam

"Elizabeth is immune to flattery because she's heard it all. Since childhood. How beautiful she is and so on. The one compliment that may buy you a little time with her is about her acting. If she thinks you're sincere. She has almost a radar for spotting phonies. But the quality of her acting, that interests her."   —designer and friend Halston

"Unlike the vast majority of her peers Elizabeth didn't have to change her name for the movies. She loves finding out what celebrities' real names are . . . if it's an unusual or funny moniker, she'll often call that person by their real name from then on."

—actor Ray Stricklyn

"My birth name was Fluck. . . . When I met Elizabeth Taylor she was aware of that. We shook hands and she said, 'Diana, what a lovely name.' I'd recently been in a circus-themed picture with Joan Crawford, whom Elizabeth detested. She moved in closer and asked, 'How the fluck did you manage to get on with old Joan?'"   —British actress Diana Dors

"Of course it bloody hurts. What do you think, sh--head?!"

> —Richard Burton, asked by a reporter whether it hurt that ET was dallying with businessman Peter Darmanin (while RB was dallying with Susan Hunt)

"Those two, always they were trying to make each other jealous. And always it worked."

> —French actress Capucine

"I don't assume Miss Taylor is too happy about it. I personally am not unhappy about it and frankly don't care."

> —Formula 1 racing champion James Hunt, on his ex-wife Susan wedding Richard Burton

"During her [John] Warner period Elizabeth Taylor announced she henceforth wanted to be called Elizabeth Warner. Said it was her 'destiny as a woman.' Not even just to add his name to hers, à la Farrah Fawcett-Majors, but to obliterate her name and identity. I asked myself what is she *on*? Is it even *her* idea? . . . Of course she was soon back to being Elizabeth Taylor."

> —writer Dominick Dunne

"She's a creature of whims. But stubborn. Elizabeth will stick to her whim, come hell or high water. Until the next whim comes along."

> —actor Farley Granger

"When she's happy and has self-esteem, Elizabeth watches her weight so others can watch her and be happy. When she's not happy, she overeats. . . . Hubby John Warner is a Virginian. He's used to chicken and ham. . . . Miss Taylor has developed a passion for Southern fried chicken."

> —columnist Joan Wilson

"Scarcely a year passes without a doctor's emergency visit to Elizabeth Taylor. This year [1978] a medic was called to remove a chicken-wing bone that had lodged in her throat."

—ET biographer C. David Heymann

"In time, Elizabeth realized how far apart she and Warner were. One of their biggest fights was about the military draft, which John felt should be limited to males. Elizabeth insisted women could fight too—and was her own best evidence."

—film producer Daniel Melnick

"The 1980s see Miss Taylor returning to her old self, which invariably includes the movies. She's dropped forty pounds and looks fantastic . . . said the gain had been due to her politicized life as Mrs. John Warner. 'It was so boring. That's why I put on so much weight.'"

—columnist Richard Gully

"No, Elizabeth, you can't take the elephant home."

—Mexican attorney and boyfriend Victor Gonzalez Luna during a trip to Asia, where ET pointed at an elephant and said she wanted it

"Hmm. One carat, I see. You *are* on a diet, aren't you, luv?"

—Richard Burton when ET showed him Victor Luna's engagement ring, actually a $300,000 16.5 carat sapphire-and-diamond ring from Cartier

"Elizabeth fainted and then she asked me to go and be with her . . . I knew she would be devastated, shattered. But I didn't expect her to become completely hysterical. I could not get her to stop crying. She was completely out of control. I realized then how deeply she was tied to this man, how vital a role he had played in her life. And I realized I could never have that special place in her heart she keeps for Burton. For me, the romance was over, and I told Elizabeth that."
—Victor Luna, upon the death of Richard Burton in 1984

"Ever after Richard, poor Elizabeth was remembering him. So many things reminded her. She realized that with him she'd experienced her peak, romantically and professionally. The men after him were just there, just necessary background, like a radio you leave on for distraction."   —MGM colleague Gene Kelly

"Having done it myself, I don't think it's so unusual to marry the same man twice. You don't stop loving him after you break up. With time, you find you miss him and that despite the compromises it was and is worth it. So you remarry."
—Natalie Wood on ET and RB

"When passion fades, eyesight improves and reality can set in . . . I think Richard and Elizabeth clung to each other closely when the world was against them for leaving their spouses. Once they made it legal and reached the top and were accepted as a couple and had all the things money could buy, they probably started in on each other."
—costar John Goodman (*The Flintstones*)

"Their tempers and insecurities kept breaking them up. One thing that didn't help was when they did *Private Lives*. It was for Elizabeth's company, so she was the producer and technically the boss. Richard got offered a choice movie role by John Huston, who'd directed him in *Night of the Iguana*. But Elizabeth rightly held him to his contract, so he couldn't do the movie [Albert Finney did]. Elizabeth explained she didn't want to disappoint their fans—the idea was Liz and Dick in *Private Lives*, not Elizabeth and somebody else. She was committed to the play . . . he'd long ago lost interest in the stage, but she'd recently discovered it. Richard just wanted to remain a big fat movie star."

—Maureen Stapleton, who costarred with ET in her prior play, *The Little Foxes*

"Richard Burton was horrified [during *Private Lives*] the few times that Liz Taylor was absent from the production. A stand-in would go on in her place, and in the middle of a scene people actually got up and walked out. Burton was mortified. People wanted to see *her*."

—critic Rex Reed

"I didn't think their second marriage would last ten minutes. But I could also see that they seemed to need each other. When he was there, she seemed to hate him. When he was away, she couldn't bear to be without him. They were often at each other's throats and there was plenty of hard-core swearing on both sides."

—the couple's bodyguard Brian Haynes

"Elizabeth took it very hard when Richard married a younger woman. Almost as if to get back at her. She couldn't very well do the same without looking foolish. Not yet. Later she did marry a younger man, and that fizzled rather quickly."

—Joan Collins

"Richard up and married Suzy Hunt. She was twenty-seven and unlike Elizabeth was tall and blonde. Soft-spoken . . . somebody Richard could probably dominate. How much more could he have done to irk Elizabeth than marrying her?"
—Peter Lawford

"*Private Lives* was a box-office hit but it estranged them. Burton's sense of professionalism hated that Taylor was always late to the theatre while he was always on time. Since he was markedly cool towards her, Elizabeth flaunted her beau Victor Luna backstage. So then *he* flaunted Susan Hunt. Increasingly jealous of Luna and resentful of Elizabeth, Richard married Susan without warning Liz. She was genuinely shocked and extremely hurt that Richard had acted so rashly . . . she'd thought making him jealous would bring him back."
—hairdresser Kenneth

"After Suzy Hunt he married Sally Hay . . . and would have kept remarrying had he not died at 58. Richard's ego or image required a woman by his side. He was not homophobic, except sometimes while drunk. But one reason he drank was embarrassment over his relationship with Philip Burton. Richard's c.v. read that he was a mere boy when he lived with his teacher. The fact came out that he was a young man. Not till after 2000 or so did you find that fact in some books, while the popular media entirely evades the subject. Plus the merger with Liz Taylor totally overshadowed how or why Richard Jenkins became Richard Burton."
—Hollywood agent Dick Clayton

"Elizabeth helped Richard Burton feel less ashamed of having had gay sex. He told *Time* or some other magazine his theory that perhaps most actors are 'latent homosexuals' who drink to banish the feeling. Elizabeth was unable to make Richard less ashamed of being an actor. To draw attention away from it, he spent prodigiously. As though he were only acting to keep his wife in luxury."   —Scottish director Ronald Neame

"Elizabeth was convinced where there wasn't any jealousy, there wasn't any love. Not that Richard isn't a jealous man himself. He's more apt to simmer and stew, usually in alcohol. Elizabeth's more apt to want to gouge her rival's eyes out."
—Burton's brother Graham Jenkins

"A great irony that Philip Burton outlived [to age ninety] his most celebrated pupil. . . . He was of course remembered in Richard's will."
—Richard Burton biographer Alexander Walker

"It's not always how the fans or followers imagine. Laurel and Hardy are buried in separate cemeteries, as are Juan and Eva Peron in Argentina. Richard Burton and Elizabeth Taylor are in separate countries, and he's not in Wales, he's in Switzerland. . . . For years there was speculation that she would be buried in the Westwood cemetery in Los Angeles, where her father and mother were. I didn't believe it for a second. Marilyn Monroe is the reigning star at Westwood. It houses a galaxy of stars, but Marilyn is tops there. . . . Instead, Elizabeth chose Forest Lawn, way over in Glendale."
—actress Jayne Meadows

"If Richard and Elizabeth had just been more considerate toward each other, the way they were with most people. But they derived a sado-masochistic pleasure in goading each other, at first privately, but over the years increasingly publicly."

—Mr. Blackwell, who designed clothes for ET until he put her on his Worst-Dressed list

"I recall that Elizabeth had a quick temper, but I am basically placid. When she started to pick a quarrel I used to infuriate her by refusing to be drawn into a ding-dong row. 'You're so goddamn British!' she used to rage. 'I'll bet if I told you I'd taken a lover your only reaction would be to ask him round for afternoon tea!'"

—second husband Michael Wilding

"Elizabeth Taylor, solo or with Burton, could swamp fellow actors, publicity-wise. Without meaning to. It cost them some friendships and turned several of their peers against them. Jealousy. . . . Elizabeth couldn't help being a juggernaut. Among stars she was a star. I do know of one occasion when she felt compelled to apologize."

—British actress Coral Browne

"I learned that Rachel [Roberts, actress wife of Rex Harrison] and Rex were standing near their car after the [premiere of their film] being photographed when suddenly the photographers saw Elizabeth appearing and abandoned the two Harrisons. Rachel in a red Welsh fury screamed 'I'm the star of this f---ing show not that f---ing Elizabeth Taylor etc.' The photographers took no notice."

—from Richard Burton's diary entry for October 22, 1968

"I love what Liz Taylor said when she was asked about feuds and fellow actresses. She said the only people she feuded with were her husbands."
—Farrah Fawcett

"She's not the best interview subject, because some things she hardly talks about. Like she's so protective of Montgomery Clift. Or much about her marriages. Our magazine [*Andy Warhol's Interview*, later just *Interview*] had a list of prepared questions but mostly she talked about whatever she wanted. Most other interviewers aren't good with her because mostly what they want is to meet Elizabeth Taylor and look at her."
—Andy Warhol

"One of the saddest yet angriest moments of Elizabeth's life was being barred from Richard Burton's funeral by the, I'd say, rather vindictive and jealous widow [Sally] Hay. She'd been Richard's assistant. He didn't court Hay, he just married her. And like many or most wives she then became an unpaid assistant."   —theater producer Lore Noto

"Elizabeth Taylor agreed with Sally Hay that if she showed up at the funeral, the media would descend upon that grave and private occasion like locusts."
—costar Michael Caine (*X, Y and Zee*)

"After Mike Todd died Elizabeth seriously considered giving up acting and moving to Hawaii where her brother Howard lived. . . . She was big into tanning. Her mother disapproved because it's wrinkle-making and she preferred Elizabeth's creamy white complexion."
—Truman Capote

"Another significant source of income for Miss Taylor is Todd-AO. As in American Optical. It was a filmmaking process Mike Todd invested in and she inherited. Whenever possible, her films were made using Todd-AO. . . . Like that song from *Evita* says, 'and the money kept rolling in from every side.'"

—columnist James Bacon

"Liz and Dick were amassing so much income at a time of very steep taxes that they had to set up personal corporations and multi-national tax shelters and establish Swiss residency. Elizabeth, who was British born, returned and took up British citizenship, but quietly, so as not to alienate American audiences."

—Hollywood business manager Morgan Maree

"The lady wasn't one for self-pity. When her career choices finally and inevitably narrowed she made the best of what was available and opened up two new avenues—championing a cure for AIDS and starting a perfume business. She kept busy and vital and did heroic work."

—Julia Roberts

"Elizabeth Taylor and Rock Hudson were friends and shared personal memories of making *Giant* and of Michael Wilding, etc. But Elizabeth was closer to [three-time costar] Montgomery Clift, and a big reason she became an AIDS activist was her conviction that had Monty lived he could easily have contracted HIV. Rock Hudson was the catalyst, but Elizabeth did it for Monty and in essence for all her gay friends."

—ex-actor and Monty intimate Jack Larson

"While the Reagan administration did literally nothing to fight AIDS, Liz Taylor was trying to launch the anti-AIDS bandwagon. She actually received death threats . . . and some of her celebrity friends crawled into the woodwork or belittled her. Sinatra called it one of her 'lame-dog causes.' But then, he didn't hide his affinity for gangsters and mafia, did he?"   —ex-actor Kerwin Mathews (*The 7th Voyage of Sinbad*)

"When she planned the first gala fundraiser against AIDS Ms. Taylor asked Frank Sinatra to participate. He refused to have anything to do with it, thinking it was a 'gay disease.' Their friendship cooled after that, eventually into nothing. Most people in the business knew about it, but Elizabeth Taylor didn't make Sinatra's bigotry public. I think it should be known. And now it is."
—Sir Elton John

"Taylor never disclosed Michael Wilding's bisexuality. Maybe because of her two Wilding sons. She advocated that gay people come out and be free from hiding and pretense, but she respected if somebody chose to stay in the closet . . . like her supposed boyfriend Malcolm Forbes."   —publicist Andrea Jaffe

"Unfortunately there is some hypocrisy. Elizabeth Taylor has helped lessen the stigma of living with and dying from AIDS. But when it's a famous friend like Malcolm Forbes she goes silent about his cause of death. . . . I've heard her official line is that Michael Wilding, her ex-husband, was 'straight.' I know he was more closeted in Hollywood than in England. . . . In other words, nothing wrong with being gay or bi, but if it's somebody close to you, they weren't."   —Screen Actors Guild president Patty Duke

"Rumors persisted that Forbes died of AIDS, and it was a strong possibility. He had the money and connections to cover it up. Elizabeth is no stranger to wealth, but when asked how he died she either doesn't let on or says she doesn't know, which is somewhat possible."

—writer-director Garry Marshall

"A friend of mine was at Elizabeth's home on Nimes Road [in Bel Air] one night. Five or six people were watching *A Place in the Sun*. There came a scene—I think a court scene—which had Montgomery Clift, Raymond Burr, and Keefe Brasselle all in a row. Elizabeth cried out, 'My God! All three were gay!' She shook her head and muttered, 'If the public only *knew* . . .' And there are so many scenes and movies where that's the case—nobody knew it then, hardly anyone knows it now."

—agent turned nightclub owner Robert Hussong

"I find it funny, if not humorous, that pro-gay Elizabeth Taylor all but insured John Warner's ascent to the Senate, where he remains and where he consistently votes against gay marriage and gay-rights bills."
—Robert L. Spencer, who with longtime partner Mr. Blackwell designed clothes for ET

"Acting is a vocation. Stardom is an addictive way of life. The longer one is at it, the more difficult. The more desperate a star becomes. Several of Elizabeth's choices, personal and professional, have been made from desperation. And frustration. I gave up the crazy competition years ago."

—Jean Simmons

"For a particular anniversary I accompanied Elizabeth to the cemetery where her parents are. . . . On its opposite side lies James Aubrey, who headed CBS and MGM. We walked over to his small marker, inscribed 'A Man Among Men'—ironic, because he was bisexual. Aubrey was known in the business as The Smiling Cobra. He was widely disliked, which Elizabeth knew. She didn't know that Keefe Brasselle, after he left acting, became Aubrey's assistant and lover. Both men had wives, and I think they were bi, not gay. Elizabeth was fascinated, she asked if I knew anything more about them."

—Roddy McDowall

"Sara Taylor was a pill. Old but feisty, and very proud of what she believed she'd made out of her daughter. Toward the end, she lived in a condo at the Sunrise Country Club complex in Rancho Mirage, near Palm Springs. A number of gay retired MGM actors lived there and served as her escorts when she went out. Sara's entrée and carte blanche to everything was 'I'm Elizabeth Taylor's mother,' which she wasn't at all shy about saying . . . as often as she had to, for instance to get into a swanky restaurant where she hadn't made a reservation."

—Brooks Hallman, former Sunrise resident

"Sara was very much of her era. I was present when a colleague remarked something about Elizabeth Taylor being Jewish and it soon being Hanukkah. Sara Taylor drew herself up and pronounced, 'My daughter is *not* Jewish.' She even repeated it. Nor was Mrs. Taylor lacking other bigotries, as well."

—Fred Ebb of the composer-lyricist team Kander & Ebb

"This may be apocryphal. I heard it from a boyfriend of Malcolm Forbes, who liked guys who liked motorcycles. Liz Taylor's mother was doing an interview with a foreign wire service. Toward its conclusion, the journalist brought up several of Elizabeth's gay buddies. Finally he wondered aloud if Liz's father himself had been gay. The old lady didn't hear well, so the interviewer repeated it. There was a long silence. The man didn't know if Sara Taylor had heard or was ignoring his question. Finally she said, 'My late husband was not very sexually inclined.' Perhaps the long pause was to devise an answer that didn't say yes and didn't say no." —Charles Pierce, drag artiste

"What was Elizabeth Taylor thinking when she backed a Republican for the Senate who was anti women's rights, etc.? She campaigned for him, raised funds for him, she was terribly effective. I think it was tunnel vision . . . there was a contest on, called an election, and Elizabeth was still in the limelight after Richard Burton and wanted desperately to win. Except of course *he* won. She didn't."
—Jane Fonda

"After her marriages to Richard, Elizabeth needed someone or something high-profile to stay a big celebrity. Film roles were scarce and she didn't have the discipline for any more theater work. She needed a VIP consort or husband, or one she could help make into a VIP. Politicking was new to her, so for the time being it was fun and interesting. But soon she was just smiling in public while arguing in private, and enjoying overeating but miserable about its results." —ghostwriter William F. Dufty

"She's a warm, cuddly blanket that I love to snuggle up to and cover myself with. I can confide in her and trust her. In my business you can't trust anyone. . . . Elizabeth is also like a mother—and more than that, she's a friend."
—Michael Jackson

"After Michael Jackson became big on his own he reached out to several older female stars . . . Kate Hepburn, Sophia Loren, Jane Fonda, Liz Taylor. When the molestation charges about the young boys surfaced and he started paying millions to quiet them, the ladies, even old friend Diana Ross, distanced themselves from him. The one who didn't was Elizabeth Taylor. She was more than ready to not be one of the bunch and to have him 'court' her with flattery, publicity, and expensive gifts. Liz always liked to be considered hip and up-to-date. His gifts continued . . . and she stayed loyal."
—costume designer Ray Aghayan

"I'm surprised and disappointed that Miss Taylor, as the mother of two sons, lends her public support to an adult male who is habitually enamored of boys—none of Michael Jackson's accusers have been girls. His is an unhealthy personality, as is her willingness to excuse each and any of his eccentricities and aberrations."
—novelist Muriel Spark (*The Driver's Seat*)

"Jackson makes no secret of his maintaining a shrine to Elizabeth Taylor at his Neverland ranch. It is doubtful that the veteran actress considers it idolatry."
—Morley Safer (*60 Minutes*)

"She must be off her nut . . . I can just imagine what Richard [Burton] would say about her describing Michael Jackson as 'the most normal man I know.'" —Peter O'Toole

"Oscar-winning actor Red Buttons remains a topical funnyman. His most famous joke is 'Only in America can a poor black boy like Michael Jackson grow up to become a rich white woman.' Insiders confirm that the first time Elizabeth Taylor heard the joke she couldn't help but laugh. Subsequently, she says it isn't funny." —columnist James Bacon

"It has to be said: you could buy your way to Elizabeth. She was at heart a collector . . . of jewels, art, valuable things. Her pretend-romance with Malcolm Forbes began when he donated $1 million to her AIDS foundation. Later, he jokingly asked what it would take for her to visit his bedroom. She said, 'A big thing in a little blue box—from Tiffany's.'" —ET biographer C. David Heymann

"The first million-dollar check to fight AIDS was given by a Japanese philanthropist. The second by American magazine publisher Malcolm Forbes, who recruited Elizabeth Taylor to cloak his true sexuality. It was two converted Jewish women—Ms. Taylor and Dr. Mathilde Krim, wife of United Artists chief Arthur Krim—who helped start AmFAR, the American Foundation for AIDS Research. It went on to become the leading U.S. nonprofit dedicated to AIDS research and prevention." —Richard Wherrett, founding director of the Sydney Theatre Company (who died of AIDS)

"On an AIDS fund-raising junket to Japan in 1988, Elizabeth was invited aboard Malcolm Forbes's yacht, where to her dismay she was greeted by the entire crew of Robin Leach's television show *Lifestyles of the Rich and Famous*. She never appeared on television without pay, but the publicity-mad Malcolm had set a trap. She adroitly sidestepped it by refusing to let Leach's cameramen near her until Forbes agreed to give Elizabeth an Erte painting."

—ET biographer Ellis Amburn

"Elizabeth Taylor organized the first APLA [AIDS Project Los Angeles] 'Commitment to Life' dinner in 1985. Rock Hudson had died that year, and not until then did Ronald Reagan, the president, utter the word 'AIDS'—five years into the epidemic. That dinner raised $1.3 million, more money in one night than the government's CDC [Centers for Disease Control and Prevention] had spent in its entire first year."

—writer-producer Marvin Jones

"Even America's fashion industry hesitated to acknowledge or to confront AIDS. Elizabeth Taylor was part of AmFAR's 'To Care Is to Cure' fundraiser. They wanted designer Calvin Klein to lend his support but despite several requests he wouldn't. Klein, who was then in the closet, agreed to show up only after Dr. Mathilde Krim said Elizabeth Taylor would be his date if he helped."

—European designer Karl Lagerfeld

"It wasn't widely publicized that the granddaughter of billionaire J. Paul Getty, whose grandson was kidnapped and had his ear cut off, contracted AIDS. Or that the young lady was Elizabeth Taylor's daughter-in-law. Elizabeth took Aileen Getty under her wing and helped to ease her final days."

—columnist Radie Harris

"I don't think anyone else could have done it. Someone in a leadership position—a president or a first lady—could have told the country, 'Do the right thing.' But no one in power rose to the moral occasion. The cause needed a woman at the pinnacle. Because openly gay men are not given the respect that they are due. And if a straight man speaks up on a gay issue, his orientation becomes suspect. Elizabeth was perfect for the role. And I think she knew that."

—Michael Gottlieb, M.D., immunologist, AIDS pioneer, and Rock Hudson's doctor

"Elizabeth makes magnificent use of her celebrity in battling AIDS and fundraising for the cause. She told me, 'If people want to come to an AIDS event to see whether I'm fat or thin, pretty or not, or really have violet eyes, then great, just come. My fame finally makes sense to me.'"

—columnist Liz Smith

"France has honored Elizabeth Taylor with the prestigious ribbon of the Legion of Honor. It is deserved. She is the kind of American that French culture appreciates."

—couturier Yves Saint Laurent

"When Queen Elizabeth II created her Dame Elizabeth, she was delighted. Elizabeth had dual citizenship and enjoyed being both English and American. . . . She joked that she'd always been a great dame. She didn't mind the word if it was affectionate or in tribute."

—Sir Ian McKellen

"Those weren't good years [1997 and 1998] for Elizabeth. She let herself become housebound. Depression and physical ailments brought her down to where she developed agoraphobia. I helped get her out of the house. We dated, which took her out of herself. She's great company and a good friend."

—Rod Steiger

"Elizabeth thought Beverly Hills of all places should certainly have and support an animal shelter. She was considering a fundraiser but then she had a [health] relapse and another operation. . . . In the late '90s she fell in her bedroom and broke her back. For the second time. The pain was tremendous . . . the long healing period was made worse by the prescription of only moderate pain medication, to avoid becoming addicted again."

—Evelyn Keyes, actress and ex-wife of John Huston

"Elizabeth had a Collie puppy, Nellie, descended from the legendary Lassie. She asked Larry [Fortensky] to care for it while she was out of town on AIDS business. He took Nellie into his bedroom but was negligent about taking her outside to relieve herself, and so she did so all over the room. He became angry and began cursing the dog. He locked her in her traveling container, which she had long ago outgrown, with no food or water. The dog whimpered for many hours until she was rescued by one of the household staff. When Elizabeth found out, she became extremely upset and a big argument resulted."

—ET biographer J. Randy Taraborrelli

"Elizabeth Taylor's most constant companion is her little white dog Sugar, who has accompanied her on dates with actor Rod Steiger and her Beverly Hills dentist Dr. Cary Schwartz. . . . Don't count on Liz taking a ninth matrimonial plunge. She now feels the only people who should get married are gay people."

—columnist Janet Charlton

"Elizabeth Taylor was delighted when Michael Jackson introduced her to his widely photographed little chimpanzee, Bubbles. . . . A sad ending to that, for years later, when Bubbles was older and no longer photogenic, he was abandoned. Hardly anybody printed that at the time . . . I don't know if Elizabeth was aware of it. If she was, she might have done something about it. I say *might*."

—*The Simpsons* co-creator and animal advocate Sam Simon

"Like more stars than the public imagines, Elizabeth Taylor spent part of her final years in a wheelchair. But publicly. . . . She had two hip replacement surgeries. Then one had to be redone . . . she was left with one leg slightly shorter than the other. What she went through and endured boggles the mind." —costume designer Arnold Scaasi

"Who could have predicted these two antagonists would ever share the screen? Yet in 2001 we have the historic pairing of Elizabeth Taylor and Debbie Reynolds. Add to the mix Shirley MacLaine and Joan Collins. What a cast! Dismally, they're wasted on the *small* screen in a dismal little project with the mocking title *These Old Broads*. How the mighty have fallen."
—mystery writer Ruth Rendell

"Despite its star power *These Old Broads* was barely watchable. The script was banal, vulgar, and disjointed. In a supporting role, Elizabeth Taylor played a screechy New Yawk–accented super-agent based on Sue Mengers whose clients are the other three ladies. Poor health and limited mobility required many of Taylor's scenes to be shot in bed. It was a colorful though not very ballyhooed end to a storied career—Elizabeth Taylor's final acting gig." —producer David Wolper

"Her reactions and speech became more peculiar. In interviews she'd always spoken calmly and in measured tones. But in later years she might whoop or bug her eyes and sometimes say irrational things or non sequiturs. This, as much as her health or puffy face or longer chin, put her out of the running for leading roles and most secondary ones."
—casting director Monica Velasquez

"How sad that [Elizabeth Taylor] would outlive her career. . . . Elizabeth let it be known that she wished to continue acting, but . . . was also uninsurable. She did not become a recluse or bitter, she still did what she could, she was still social and active. Basically, she refused to give up."
—producer Ismail Merchant

"It may have been bravado, but Elizabeth Taylor said she intended to live to a hundred. Her mother had nearly made it. . . . Her father [four years younger than Sara] didn't reach seventy-five, so when Elizabeth did, she celebrated a special birthday. In light of her beleaguered medical history and how she'd nearly died while young and in middle age, how nearly incredible and lucky for us that her heart kept going until it was seventy-nine."
—director Leslie H. Martinson (who lived to 101)

"Elizabeth Taylor died in 2011. Her earnings in 2012, including estate auctions, came to $210 million."
—celebrity maven Perez Hilton

"In 2015 five of Elizabeth Taylor's grandchildren presented New York Democratic Congressman Jose Serrano, advocate of needle-exchange programs, with the Inaugural Elizabeth Taylor Legislative Leadership Award."
—Los Angeles TV news anchor Robert Kovacik

In Her Own Words

"I look forward to growing old with him."

—after wedding Conrad Nicholson Hilton Jr., her first husband

"We're truly and deeply in love."   —on her second marriage, to Michael Wilding

"I've just had my second baby and I want to be able to share fully in both of my children's lives. I'm happily married to my second husband, and he will carry on with his acting career while I spend more time at home. I've been acting since as long as I can remember, so I think I'm due an early retirement."

—at age twenty-three in 1955, by which time she'd appeared in twenty movies

"We started as husband and wife, but it ended like brother and sister."

—after divorce number two

"The Elizabeth Taylor who's famous, the one on film, really has no depth or meaning to me. She's a totally superficial working thing, a commodity. I really don't know what the ingredients of the image are exactly—just that it makes money."

"This marriage is forever."   —after wedding Mike Todd, husband number three

"I'm not taking anything away from Debbie Reynolds, because she never really had it."
   —hinting at the near-sexless marriage she supposedly broke up

"I'm working to make this last."   —after wedding husband number four, Eddie Fisher

"Eddie is so much fun to be with . . . we have a great time."
   —but pal Truman Capote noted, "We used to make jokes about him.
   We called him the Bus Boy. He was so boring! But I felt sorry for
   him too. He was so in love with her, and she was so rude to him."

"There's not a decent stone in here."
   —to Eddie Fisher, about a $50,000 diamond necklace he gave her

"We were spit at! . . . What used to kill us (she and Richard Burton) was when people
would say, 'We don't care what they do in private life, but do they have to air their dirty
linen in public?' God, we were doing everything we could not to make it public."

"I suppose I have behaved immorally."
   —about her husbands Eddie Fisher and Richard Burton leaving
   their wives and children for her

"I know this will last forever."   —on marriage number five, to Richard Burton

"The public takes an animal delight in putting somebody at the top and then tearing them into little bits. But I have never in my life believed in fighting back to 'cure' my public image . . . I'm not going to answer for an image created by hundreds of people who do not know what's true or false."

"I have learned, however, that there's no deodorant like success."

"I wish I could tell you of my pure animal pleasure of you."

—from a letter to Richard Burton

"How sweet . . . though he didn't say he wanted to be my hand."

—after Andy Warhol announced he'd like to be reincarnated as a diamond on the hand of ET

"I feel as though I'm only the custodian of my jewelry. When I die and they go off to auction I hope whoever buys them gives them a really good home."

"I can believe it."

—after hearing that director Edward Dmytryk, who directed them both, declared ET an "all-around stronger" individual than Richard Burton

"He calls me Lumpy and I call him Pockface." —her and Burton's pet names for each other

"Sometimes I call him Charlie Charm. Women do seem to go for him."   —about Burton

"Get that woman out of my bed!"

—upon hearing that Burton had been unfaithful to her after eight years (with *Bluebeard* costar Nathalie Delon)

"This is for Nathalie."

—to a friend, showing off a large sapphire ring gifted her by Burton after his one-night stand

"Maybe we loved each other too much. . . . Pray for us."

—about the end of her marriage to Richard Burton

"This time will be better than the last."   —about her second marriage to Burton

"That was a kind of a phase in my life, a kind of camp and fun phase. Maybe my values have matured with my age."

—when asked whether, while married to politician John Warner, she would wear the jewels given her by Richard Burton

"I haven't gone out to pasture. I haven't given up . . . I know my own identity, not as a movie star, but as a woman."

—after wedding number seven, to sixth husband John Warner

"We're going to make this marriage work."

—on marriage number seven

"Don't you raise that all-commanding, domineering hand to me!"
—to Republican Warner, who tried to keep her from voicing her
support for the Equal Rights Amendment

"It's no fun breaking your back twice and almost dying twice . . . and having to ingest a steady stream of pain killers. Drugs are dangerous, whether prescribed or not."

"The entire process of tearing down and rebuilding on a solid foundation of self-awareness makes it possible for almost anyone to conquer those demons."
—after her first rehab visit to the Betty Ford Center

"We have different backgrounds but we fell into drug dependency and in love at Betty Ford."   —after meeting construction worker Larry Fortensky

"I'm getting married for good this time."
—after wedding for the eighth and final time

"If I ever get married again, and I won't, I should have my head examined. As far as I'm concerned, only gay people should get married. It doesn't seem to work for heterosexuals."

"I'm through with marriage, but I'm not through with men."   —after her final divorce

"Oh, yes. I wish I could bottle it, like my perfume."
—when asked if she was proud of her taste in men

"I am my own commodity. I am my own industry."

"I am suing ABC television network because they are doing a story of my life which is completely fictionalized unless there was somebody under the carpet or under the bed during my 50 years."

"It's bad enough that people are dying of AIDS, but no one should die of ignorance."
 —testifying before the Labor, Health and Human Services Senate Subcommittee in 1986

"Your participation in the dinner would mean a great deal to not only the American Foundation for AIDS Research but also to people like me who are critically concerned with the ever-growing impact of the AIDS epidemic. . . . P.S. My love to you, Nancy, I hope to see you soon, E."
              —trying to shame President Ronald Reagan into attending an AIDS fund-raiser

"I don't think President Bush is doing anything at all about AIDS. In fact, I'm not even sure if he knows how to spell 'AIDS.'"

"Passion is the name of my first perfume but is also the way that I live . . . I stopped being quietly repressed when I was very young. Who and what I care about, I feel deeply—with genuine passion."

ACKNOWLEDGMENTS

As always, Ronald Boze supplied the most help, with the welcome bonus of clippings galore via Linda Fresia.

I thank my agents Stephen A. Fraser and Jennifer De Chiara, editor Rick Rinehart, editor Ellen Urban, and publicist Jessica Kastner.

Also Dr. Jeffrey Brettler, Andrew Budgell, Tyler Cassity, Charles Coffman, Rick Egusquiza, E. J. Fleming, Jim Key, Robert Kovacik, Jerry Kunz and Richard Winger, Eric Larson, Chad Oberhausen, Shawn Pelofsky, Andrew Pincus, Aimee Rand, Greg Schreiner, Roy Stone, Marilyn Taniguchi, and Harry Walders.

Interested Taylor fans may wish to visit, among other quality websites, DameElizabethTaylor.com, fanpop.com, and the Elizabeth Taylor AIDS Foundation at etaf.com.

PHOTO CREDITS

Photos courtesy of Photofest: Pages 10, 15, 24, 34, 41, 42, 49, 55, 61, 66, 71, 76, 81, 86, 95, 103, 113, 134, 140, 148, 153; Photos courtesy of MGM/Photofest: Pages iv, 5, 29, 90; Photos courtesy of Paramount/Photofest: Page 38; Photos courtesy of Warner Bros./Photofest: Page 108; Photos courtesy of Columbia Pictures/Photofest: Page 126 (Photographer: Bob Penn); Photos courtesy of Twentieth Century Fox/Photofest: Pages 130 (Photographer: Bob Penn), 158

ABOUT THE AUTHOR

Boze Hadleigh is the author of two dozen books, including *Marilyn Forever*. The *Los Angeles Times* labeled him "a pop culture dynamo." Elizabeth Taylor contributed the blurb "It's all too true!" to his book *Holy Matrimony!* Hadleigh speaks five languages, has visited sixty-three countries, holds a master's degree in journalism, and has won on *Jeopardy!* He lives in Beverly Hills, California, and Sydney, Australia.

By the same author:

Marilyn Forever
Celebrity Feuds!
Life's a Pooch
Holy Cow!
Hollywood Gays
An Actor Succeeds
Broadway Babylon
492 Great Things about Being Italian
Hollywood Lesbians: From Garbo to Foster